To Uncle Paddy.

HAPPY CHRISTMAS 2014

I Hope you Enjoy this
Book.

Love Deeds xx

G000068642

FROM CLERY'S CLOCK TO *WANDERLY WAGON*
Irish History You Weren't Taught at School

Damian Corless, a journalist and a former editor of *Magill* and *In Dublin*, currently contributes to the *Irish Independent*. He has written comedy sketches for BBC TV's classic *Big Train* and RTÉ's award-winning *Stew*. His acclaimed books include *GUBU Nation*, *The Greatest Bleeding Hearts Racket in the World* and *Looks Like Rain*, a lively romp through 9,000 years of dependably undependable Irish weather.

FROM CLERY'S CLOCK TO *WANDERLY WAGON*

Irish History You Weren't Taught at School

Damian Corless

The Collins Press

For Sophie, Ollie, Max and Caitlin.

First published in 2014 by
The Collins Press
West Link Park
Doughcloyne
Wilton
Cork

Reprinted 2014

A CIP record for this book is available from the British Library.

ISBN: 978-1-84889-227-9

Design and typesetting by Hugh Adams, AB3 Design.
Typeset in Bembo, Foundry Sterling and Trajan.

Printed in Poland by Białostockie Zakłady Graficzne SA.

CONTENTS

INTRODUCTION

The Book of Kells and Mister Tayto. The uilleann pipes and 20 Major. Clery's Clock and *Wanderly Wagon*. All of these things are part of what we are – or, in some cases, part of what we were – and all of them are to be found amongst the 101 objects gathered together in this volume. You might call it a What's What of Ireland.

They appear in no particular order, and with no particular regard for whether they might be pigeonholed as high art or low culture. Each has been chosen purely on its merits as an object with an entertaining – and hopefully a surprising – story to tell about Ireland and the Irish.

If this book is even half as much fun to read as it was to write, I think I can promise a highly rewarding rummage through the nation's brimming oddments drawer.

Damian Corless
2014

1: THE HALF-CROWN COIN

Mrs C. of Harrogate informed the Taoiseach that he and his people were a shower of 'cowardly skunks'.

IN 1926 THE NOBEL LAUREATE and Senator W. B. Yeats was appointed chairman of the committee charged with selecting a distinctly Irish coinage for the young Free State. The committee opted for animal designs, with the most 'noble or dignified types' to grace the higher denominations and 'the more humble types' for the lower ones. The horse was designated the 'most noble' of Irish beasts and assigned to the new State's most valuable coin, the half-crown, worth two shillings and sixpence

One reason for the horse's high standing with the Irish was its ancient reputation as one of the cleverest beasts on this earth. The pooka of traditional lore even had the ability to talk. This was an exceedingly ugly black horse said to roam free at Samhain, which is now celebrated as Hallowe'en on the last day of October and marks the passage into winter. Corn, fruits and berries had to be harvested and stored by this date, since after it elapsed all was deemed bewitched and therefore poisoned. Just to be sure, the pooka's job was to gallop around the countryside urinating on any berries left on the branch.

A lack of respect for the nobility of the Irish horse sparked a hostile letter-writing campaign across the Irish Sea in 1960 following British press reports detailing Ireland's thriving export business shipping live horses to the Continent for slaughter and sale as food. Aside from writing to the letters pages of the Irish newspapers threatening a tourism boycott, Britain's outraged animal lovers targeted Taoiseach Sean Lemass.

Mrs Catherine Harber wrote from Lancashire: 'As an Irish woman by birth, I am ashamed that my native country is making money out of CRUELTY. As long as Ireland makes a profit out of cruelty and suffering, she will lose just as much in other ways. I know many people who have boycotted holidays in Ireland and rightly so. One Travel Agency who does £10,000 worth of trade with Ireland has banned it until this shocking traffic is stopped. Ireland will be the loser. In a Catholic country whose Government consists of Catholic men, it is a shameful thing that old horses, after working all their lives, should be exploited in this way and abandoned for slaughter in another country.'

Mrs D. Shipton of Surrey told Lemass: 'It seems you Irish have another vice besides being garrulous and lazy, and that is cruelty!!! If there is such a thing as reincarnation I hope you are an Irish horse in your next life, and meet the same horrible fate as these pathetic, worn out horses!!!!' Another protester, Mrs C. Coleman-Joscelyne of Harrogate, wrote to inform the Taoiseach that he and his people were a shower of 'cowardly skunks'.

Two years earlier Taoiseach Éamon de Valera was faced with a demand that was less hot and bothered but firm nonetheless. Los Angeles schoolgirl Mary Pierce wrote to the leader of the country informing him that she had entered an inter-schools 'speech contest' on the theme of The Irish Horse, but had failed to find any relevant information in her local libraries. The eighth grader asked the Taoiseach to furnish some relevant facts, advising him: 'The speech has to be five minutes long so I need lots of information.' At the Taoiseach's request the Irish equine industry supplied her with an essay on horse breeding.

Even if he'd known the coarse horse facts about the Third Marquis of Waterford, the prudish de Valera would never have wanted them bandied about a classroom in America or anywhere else. Popularly known as The Mad Marquis, Henry Beresford had the distinction of finishing a distant last as a jockey in the English Grand National, but is better remembered for squandering a huge fortune playing elaborate pranks. Once, while in London, he mischievously decided to dispense some charity to the city's poor. To this end he bought up several casks of gin and stood on the street giving half-pint measures to anyone who looked deserving and willing. By the time the Marquis had finished his charity work, drunken riots were breaking out all around. Waterford was arrested, not for the first time.

On another occasion, riding back from a race meeting, he and his rowdy crew went on a drunken rampage through the English settlement of Melton Mowbray. Stealing paint and brushes from a construction site, they are credited with giving birth to the term 'painting the town red' by doing just that, administering a coat of crimson paint to the local constable in the process.

Another time, The Mad Marquis was charged with exceeding the speed limit in a built-up area on his horse. On the day of the trial, Waterford rode his mount up the steps of the courthouse and demanded they both be let in. He insisted that the horse would have to be his chief witness, since only it knew how fast it was really going. The judge acquitted him.

The Mad Marquis died of a broken neck – falling off a horse, appropriately enough – in 1859.

2: THE SHAMROCK CAR

After the factory shut the unused parts were transported to Lake Muckno where they sleep with the fishes.

ONE OF THE WORLD'S MOST collectable motor cars, albeit for all the wrong reasons, is The Shamrock, which was manufactured in Castleblaney, County Monaghan, around the join where the 1950s met the 1960s.

According to *The Complete Catalogue of British Cars* published in the early 1960s: 'The Shamrock car was a Spike Rhiando design based on the Austin A55 engine and other components. A factory in Tralee had been acquired for the production of this glass fibre bodied car in 1959 but only a handful were produced.'

Alvin 'Spike' Rhiando was something of an international man of mystery. First making his name in the 1930s as a star of the speedway track, he was initially billed on posters and fliers as an Italian. Depending on the location, he later added American and Canadian to his list of nationalities, while some enemies put about the story that he was actually a Deptford lad from south London chancing his arm.

The school of thought that believed Rhiando was making himself up as he went along was bolstered by a series of ripping yarns he wrote in 1939 for *Topical Times* magazine. In these pieces, Spike gave gripping accounts of his multi-crash escapades racing cars in the States. Relating one hair-raising incident, he claimed that after being hurled from the cockpit of his car, he picked himself up, made some quick running repairs to the badly damaged vehicle and fought his way back to a third-place finish in the 80-lap race.

Other tall tales featured his stints as a motorbike rider on the Wall of Death and as a fearless wing-walker with Red Herman's flying circus, and stories of how he had become pally with superstars such as Jimmy Cagney and Mae West during his time as a top Hollywood stuntman. As proof of his real mettle, he recounted his adventures running guns around the Sahara until he was captured by tribesmen and had to be rescued by the French Foreign Legion.

The years immediately before the outbreak of the Second World War were the heyday of the short-lived fad of midget car racing, and Rhiando was one of its stars. His efforts to revive midget racing fell flat in the post-war period and he turned his hand to speeding 500cc cars around the circuits at Goodwood and Silverstone where he pitted his skills against the legendary Stirling Moss.

By the late 1950s, with his racing days all but behind him, Spike was brought on board an enterprise to build a big, luxury car in Ireland for the American market. The Shamrock was the brainchild of US businessmen William K. Curtis and James Conway. Curtis and Conway established a company, Shamrock Motors Limited, and earmarked a factory space in Tralee, County Kerry, as the production centre. Teething problems quickly set in, however, and the whole project was transferred to Castleblaney in Monaghan.

Early on it became blindingly obvious that, for all his undoubted prowess on the track, Spike Rhiando hadn't a clue about car design. The proportions were all wrong, leading one commentator to describe it as looking more 'like a parade float than a car'. The fibreglass body had colossal overhangs front, rear and sides with the unfortunate upshot that if the car got a puncture the rear wheels couldn't be changed without the messy business of dislocating the rear axle. Perhaps worst of all in a vehicle designed to take on the big American gas-guzzlers, the Austin A55 engine was far too puny to carry its heavy frame at any respectable speed. In the words of one US critic, The Shamrock looked 'like a small English car wearing a big American car costume'.

As production pressed ahead in Castleblaney, the owners talked about rolling out 3,000 Shamrocks in the first year on their way to a total run of 10,000. In the event, as few as eight or ten finished articles emerged before cash-flow problems and negative publicity slammed the brakes on the project. Some reports allege that after the factory shut its doors the unused parts were transported the short distance to Lake Muckno where to this day they sleep with the fishes.

Alvin 'Spike' Rhiando died in Ireland in 1975. His granddaughter Romayne spoke for more than herself when she said: 'Spike died leaving behind many unsolved mysteries which I would love to piece together.'

3: THE SOLDIER'S SONG SHEET MUSIC

The whole thing is an abomination to anyone who knows anything about music.

THE SOLDIER'S SONG BECAME Ireland's national anthem largely by default while the architects of the Free State wrestled with more pressing matters, such as restoring social harmony following a bitter civil war.

It was composed in 1907 by Peadar Kearney and Patrick Heeney and was later adopted as the marching song of the Irish Volunteers. It became one of the theme tunes of the Easter Rising and reached a wider audience in late 1916 when it was published as sheet music in New York.

Established in 1922, the Free State got by without an official national anthem for a while. However, in 1924 Sean Lester, the Director of Publicity at the Department of External Affairs, urged the government to pick a tune because 'pro-British elements' were taking advantage of its absence to sing 'God Save The King' at public functions. Lester tactfully suggested to the cabinet that while 'The Soldier's Song' was 'excellent as a revolutionary song', it was his opinion that 'both words and music are unsuitable for a national anthem'. He proposed holding a competition to pen new lyrics for Thomas Moore's melody, 'Let Erin Remember The Days of Old'.

Ruling out a competition, the government unofficially decided to have two anthems, with 'The Soldier's Song' to be played on home ground and 'Let Erin Remember' at State occasions on foreign soil. However, the *Dublin Evening Mail* picked up on the competition angle and put up the handsome sum of 50 guineas for the best new lyrics to Moore's melody. The stellar judging panel was made up of author James Stephens, playwright Lennox Robinson and living legend William Butler Yeats. When the judges declared that not one of the entries was 'worthy of fifty guineas or any portion of it', the *Mail* asked readers to pick a winner from six of the failed lyrics.

If the votes of the *Mail*'s readers had counted, Croke Park and the Aviva Stadium on match days would today reverberate with the opening lines: *God of our Ireland, by Whose hand / Her glory and her beauty grew / Just as the shamrock o'er the land / Grows green beneath thy sparkling dew*. But the media campaign fell on deaf ears and the new State muddled on with two anthems. That this could not go on was highlighted by a Dáil farce in early 1926 when a question was tabled asking the country's leader, W. T. Cosgrave, to reveal the true identity of the national anthem.

Cosgrave passed the buck to his Defence Minister, who flatly denied that military bands had been playing two different tunes purporting to be the National Anthem, even though it was a much-witnessed fact.

Taunted by the Opposition, the Minister revealed that the Army considered 'The Soldier's Song' to be the *more* official of the rival songs. That same month, July 1926, the Free State formally adopted 'The Soldier's Song' as the lone national anthem. For some, this was to saddle the Irish people with a dirge that affronted good taste.

The critics came out in force in 1933 after Peadar Kearney sued the State for ripping him off. As the Dáil voted to buy out the copyright from Kearney and the late Patrick Heeney for £980, Deputy Frank MacDermot branded their composition 'a jaunty little piece of vulgarity' and 'a cheap music hall jingle' that was 'unworthy' of representing the Irish people in song.

Deputy Richard Anthony agreed, charging that: 'Anyone with the most elementary knowledge of music ... could not for a moment suggest that the music of "The Soldier's Song" is either inspiring or even musical.' He continued: 'The whole thing is an abomination to anyone who knows anything about music. I have hopes that some musician and some poet will collaborate one day and give us a national anthem something like the "Marseillaise".'

Half a century on, 'The Soldier's Song' could still provoke a heated reaction, as was demonstrated by an incident which took place at the Drom-Na-Gre hotel in Larne, County Antrim, during the mid-1970s at the height of the Troubles.

Fronted by Dubliner Brush Shiels (some years after he'd sacked Phil Lynott from the band), southern outfit Skid Row were on the verge of sending the audience home happy after a blistering set. The promoter told them to finish the evening with the national anthem, as was customary at the time. However, after just a few chords of 'The Soldier's Song' the promoter rushed to the side of the stage screaming at Brush: 'Play The Cream! Play The Cream!'

Slightly flummoxed, the band segued into 'Sunshine of Your Love' by Eric Clapton's 1960s supergroup Cream, before riffing back into 'Amhrán na bhFiann'. As a barrage of pint glasses and bottles hurled past, it dawned on the musicians that the promoter was howling at them to play 'God Save The Queen'. The hotel's name Drom-Na-Gre wasn't Irish, as they'd supposed, but Scots-Gaelic. After the band passed the night hiding in fear of their lives, the promoter finally persuaded the local Loyalist heavies to grant them safe passage out of the area.

4: *THE QUIET MAN* POSTER

Just as the climactic fight scene reached fever pitch the screen went blank.

IN 2013 JOHN FORD'S 1952 homecoming movie *The Quiet Man* was selected by the United States Library of Congress for preservation in the archives on the grounds that it constituted a 'culturally, historically or aesthetically significant' treasure.

Ford intended the movie as his personal sentimental journey back to the land of his forebears, with his regular on-screen alter ego John Wayne cast as the flawed hero Sean Thornton. However, when Ford (born John Feeney in the State of Maine to Galwegian parents) initially pitched the plot to Hollywood studio bosses they dismissed it as 'a silly Irish story that won't make a penny'.

Ford finally won the go-ahead from Republic Pictures, but only on condition that he would first make the western *Rio Grande* with the two leads pencilled in for *The Quiet Man*, Wayne and Maureen O'Hara. The studio's case was that *Rio Grande* would be a sure-fire hit and that the money it made at the box office would subsidise the losses *The Quiet Man* was doomed to rack up. Released in 1950 *Rio Grande* did indeed prove a critical and commercial success, and in the summer of 1951 Ford and his crew landed in Cong, County Mayo, to begin shooting.

The arrival of the Hollywood dream machine in the middle of an Irish bog was a giant shot in the arm for the drowsy local economy. In the words of one newspaper: 'In Dublin they're queuing for fuel, for buses, for jobs, for nearly everything. In Cong they're queuing for crisp pound notes. A day's work as an extra pays thirty shillings.'

At the end of each day's shooting, the local men, women and children lined up for their 30 shillings each, which represented a hefty sum in an Ireland where the average weekly wage for a man was around 60 shillings or £3. Working women doing the same job as male colleagues could expect to bring home around 60 per cent of a man's pay packet.

The Quiet Man was John Ford's labour of love, but the studio bosses at Republic Pictures had warned him from the start that it must not run to more than two hours because that was as much as audience attention spans would bear. When he had 'trimmed all the fat', to use his own phrase, the movie was still nine minutes over the 120. Ford summoned the executives to view what he told them was 'the final print'.

They watched, entranced, up until the 120th minute when, just as the climactic fight scene reached fever pitch, the screen went blank and the house lights went up. Left wanting more, the chastened studio bosses relented and *The Quiet Man* took its place in popular culture as the idealised picture-postcard image of Ireland held dear as documentary truth by millions who have never set foot on the Old Sod.

5: THE TELEPHONE DIRECTORY

Women, to their shame, are specially unbusinesslike in their use of the phone.

ONE OF THE FIRST PEOPLE in history to earn a living working for a phone company was Dubliner George Bernard Shaw who was briefly employed by the Edison Telephone Company of London until it merged with Bell to become the United Telephone Company of London in 1880.

Shaw later described the episode as 'my last attempt to earn an honest living'. Having given up the day job, he went on to become the only person to date awarded both the Nobel Prize in Literature and a movie Oscar.

In 1901 the Irish newspapers were carrying adverts for the 16th edition of Sell's *Directory of Telegraphic Addresses*. Running to 1,500 pages and priced 21 shillings, the *Directory* carried every number in the British Isles and contacts for Britain's diplomatic outposts around the globe.

By 1907 the official Post Office Telephone Directory for the United Kingdom, which included all of Ireland, showed that the phone network on the island was far more developed in the industrialised northeast than elsewhere. Of 22 phone exchanges in Ireland, 16 were to be found in the counties of Antrim, Armagh,

Derry, Fermanagh and Tyrone. The remaining six exchanges were located in Dublin, Cork, Killarney, Carlow, Tipperary and Mallow. The busiest of the southern exchanges was Killarney, which served a mere 23 telephone owners. Dublin had ten subscribers while Cork had nine.

The need for improved communications brought on by the Great War led to a huge growth in the telephone network, and by the end of the conflict in late 1918 there were around 12,500 phones in the 26-county area, of which roughly half were in and around the capital.

As telephones became more widespread in the 1930s, the Irish newspapers carried instructions for their use that would be readily understood even by women. One *Irish Times* feature from 1933 began: 'Dear Mary, are you telephone conscious? I mean, when you dial a wrong number or fail to get your pennies back from Button A – or is it Button B – or spend fourpence tram fare doing a message you could do for twopence by phone, do you feel as if you had boarded a bus labelled Dalkey and asked for a ticket for Howth? If not, you ought to!'

The writer continued: 'Women, to their shame, are specially unbusinesslike in their use of the phone. They are too impatient to read the instructions pasted in public booths. It seldom occurs to them to study the official-looking, but really enthralling, introduction to a telephone directory. I even beheld one woman dial her own number on her own phone and my shrieks of laughter failed to drown the demoniac scream of the instrument which continued to announce 'line engaged' for three full minutes.'

Another newspaper column, this one addressed to 'Dear Aileen', also stressed that the phone was 'a marvellous stand-by' for the 'up-to-date housekeepers' of 1931 if only they weren't so woolly-brained. The writer pointed out: 'Beside each telephone hangs the Leabhar Seolta Teilifóna containing all the numbers likely to be required in the day's march and other information of the greatest importance to housekeepers, and yet if you were asked if you ever read the telephone directory you would probably think it the most idiotic of questions.'

Anyone reading the Dublin 01 phone directory cover to cover in the late 1980s may have been struck that the final entry seemed a tad exotic for the pre-multicultural Ireland of the day. The last man listed in the phone book was one Paddy Zyzymugry with an address at 13 Heytesbury Street close to the city centre.

Checks of the Register of Electors and other public records by one reporter failed to produce a single Zyzymugry, and even a knock of the door of No. 13 drew a blank. The truth eventually dawned. The last person in the Dublin phonebook was a nobody. Zyzymugry was the word 'zymurgy', most likely misspelled by the publishers of the phonebook and with an extra 'zy' added by the mischief maker who dreamed up the hoax.

Zymurgy is the science of fermentation used in the making of beer and wine.

6: THE CITIZENS BAND RADIO SET

The State did not like the idea of the plain people having the freedom of the airwaves.

IN JUNE 1980 THE Fianna Fáil government announced that the fee for having a phone line installed in an Irish household was to rise to £100 the following month. The new installation fee amounted to around three weeks' wages for the average worker on £35 per week. But even being able to stump up that princely sum was no guarantee of getting a phone. A government backbencher pointed out that many householders had been on the waiting list for up to seven years to have one installed. He asked if these unfortunates could now expect to be charged the £100. The Minister replied that they would only have to pay the fee as it stood at the time of their application.

The near-impossibility of getting a phone installed, unless you had the right political connections, meant that Ireland was fertile soil for the rapid spread of Citizens Band radio. Retailing at around £50, CB radio sets weren't cheap, but they were half the cost of getting a phone installed and involved no call charges, and they were mobile insofar as they could be set into the dashboards of cars, vans and lorries. The telltale sign that a vehicle had a CB transmitter/ receiver on board was the five-foot-long aerial resembling a fishing rod mounted on the roof. Users could contact each other on set frequencies, or simply surf the airwaves striking up jargon-ridden conversations with fellow 'good buddies'.

A newspaper report from July 1980 stated: 'Citizen Band (CB) base aerials and mobile aerials are becoming commonplace throughout Ireland – a reminder that CB is the fastest-growing leisuretime "industry" in the country. At the present rate of growth every third or fourth house in the country will have its own CB radio room in a few years' time.'

After giving details of an upcoming CB Jamboree in Wicklow, the correspondent signed off: 'I find one of the interesting features to be its popularity amongst auctioneers, estate agents, builders and others involved in the property industry.' In other words, before the 'brick' mobile phone beloved of the mid-1980s yuppie, there was the CB set.

The craze had spread from the United States where it began life as an instrument of civil disobedience during the oil crisis of 1973. In response to the Arab oil embargo on the West, the US government had imposed a 55mph speed limit which was strictly enforced by the highway patrols. First truckers, and then millions of ordinary motorists, installed CB sets as a means of alerting other drivers to roadblocks and ambushes laid by the 'Smokies' (police). Its appetite whetted by the 1976 novelty hit song 'Convoy', followed by a 1978 film of the same name starring Kris Kristofferson, the Irish public went CB crazy when sets began arriving in bulk towards the end of the decade.

In 1981 a reporter visited the family homestead of Mrs Bridie Egan in the remote townland of Mount Welcome, County Galway. The journalist and Mrs Egan dropped into the home of a neighbour, Seamus Clancy, which, said the report 'sports a huge aerial'. The piece continued: '[The aerial] helps him to hold CB radio conversations with women truck drivers. Seamus, we were told, has the contract to sow and cut wheat on Bord na Móna's reclaimed turf land locally, and almost all his workforce's tractors also carry Citizen's Band radios.'

The sight of CB sets flying out of the shops sent the government into a tizzy. By 1981 there were some 100,000 CB enthusiasts in the country, and the hefty sum of £2 million was being spent each year on new equipment. In a future where every household had a CB radio, why would anyone wait an eternity for the privilege of paying a fortune for a landline? From its foundation, the State had deemed the national broadcasting service to be an arm of government and a key instrument of social control. In addition to the potential loss of revenue, and the additional consideration that terrorists could pass messages using the medium, the State simply did not like the idea of the plain people having the freedom of the airwaves.

Post & Telegraphs Minister Albert Reynolds pledged to streamline the phone service and end the interminable wait. However, no sooner had he begun a recruitment drive for trainee installers than the opposition accused him of restricting the new appointments to friends of his party, Fianna Fáil.

In 1980 a National Council of CB users had been set up to lobby for the legalisation of Ireland's fastest-growing leisure pursuit and to counter government claims that 'cowboy' users were interfering with TV signals and possibly air traffic control systems too. Under popular pressure, Reynolds legalised CB, but only on the FM band. Since the vast majority of CB radio hams were using AM sets, the new rules meant an expensive upgrade and building their contact network of 'good buddies' from scratch. There was the additional killjoy factor that FM transmissions travelled far shorter distances than AM.

For many, the new game wasn't worth the candle. While CB kept on truckin' amongst truckers, as a civilian craze it had run its natural course. In a remarkably short space of time it was over and out for Ireland's good buddies.

7: THE BLACK BABIES BOX

The special relationship became the love that dare
not speak its name.

O N 6 MARCH 1957 the Irish newspapers carried a
prominent advert tailored to run for that single day. The
illustration featured two 'black babies' in conversation.

Baby One remarks: 'Teacher says that this is the day that Ghana
gets its independence.'

Baby Two replies: 'My Mammy says that this is the day we get
our Clover Skinless Pork Sausages.'

The advert would be unthinkable today, but it reflected the
iconic place of the Black Babies Box in mid-20th-century Irish
society. That place was on the counter of every newsagent, every
drapers, every grocers and every church entrance. In fact, it was
just about everywhere. The slogan 'A Penny For The Black Babies'
was as much a part of the lexicon as 'Put A Tiger In Your Tank' or
'Vote, Vote, Vote For De Valera'. It was as if the Black Babies were
the children of the thousands of Catholic priests and nuns out on
the Missions in Africa, and that the decent folk of the Irish nation
were their godparents.

Then, almost overnight sometime in the late 1970s, the boxes
vanished from sight. The sincerely felt special relationship that the
Irish people believed they had with the Black Babies became the
love that dare not speak its name.

In fact, the earliest mention of Black Babies in the Irish media appears in an 1891 edition of *The Irish Times*, and was almost certainly a straight lift from an English paper. The writer complained that London 'street hawkers' and 'gutter merchants' were doing a roaring trade by 'unblushingly thrusting' little black dolls in the faces of passers-by. There was nothing special about the dolls, but some bright spark had rebranded them as 'Lord Randolph Churchill's little black babies' and they were selling like hot cakes at a penny a pop.

The father of the future war leader Winston was, at the time, touring southern Africa, shooting lions and sending back gripping reports of his manly adventures. Upon his return from Africa, Churchill fetched up in Ireland making fierce Unionist speeches against Prime Minister Gladstone's plans to grant Home Rule. He is credited with coining the slogan, still to be heard today: 'Ulster will fight and Ulster will be right!'

The swaddling of the black babies by Irish society began in the 1930s as a proud but penniless independent nation fastened on one of the very few good news stories it had to tell – that of its missionaries. It was something warm and exotic to feel a part of. In a Lonely Hearts column from 1933, 'Black Baby' from Dublin described herself as 'a girl of exceptional ability, sincere, earnest and interesting'. After reciting a long list of personal qualities, she concluded: 'Regards her work as a stop-gap occupation until matrimony claims her.'

By the 1950s Ireland was going Black Baby crazy. Black babies were popping up as clues in *The Irish Times* crossword, top designer Sybil Connolly was using Black Baby Ribbon in her costly creations, and the exclusive Switzer's department store was selling 'Black Baby Dolls' for 23s 6d each.

In a 1954 trial of a 14-year-old Dublin boy, a judge remarked that it was 'a nice commentary' on the times when he heard from a witness that some proprietors now had to chain their Black Babies boxes to their counters. The judge asked the boy why he had stolen the box containing almost £1. When the youth replied that he'd simply wanted the money, the judge boomed: 'You wanted to rob the Black Babies!'

Two years later a pair of Wicklow men were sentenced to

two and three years of hard labour for breaking into a school and stealing coins to the value of about £1. The press reported that: 'Schoolchildren identified pennies which they had put into the Black Baby box, and which had subsequently been collected from licensed premises where Merrigan and Fitzpatrick had paid with coppers and small silver for liquor.' No indication was given as to how the schoolchildren had recognised the coins as their own.

At the very start of the 1960s Myles na gCopaleen, in his 'Cruiskeen Lawn' satirical column, confronted the nation's gombeen publicans with the accusation that their criminal endeavours included fleecing the customers, watering down the brandy and whiskey, and 'probably you regularly rifle that box for the Black Babies'.

In early 1960s a great wave of decolonisation swept Africa, and the word started coming back to Ireland that maybe the Black Babies box was beginning to seem like a remnant of an old-fashioned patronising colonialism, however well intentioned. Perhaps more hurtful were the harsher voices asserting that all those pennies in all those boxes had never been more than a drop in the ocean when it came to fixing the troubles of Africa and that the main beneficiaries were the Irish people themselves who got to feel a little better about their own fairly dismal lives.

A road paved with good intentions had come to an end but the message took more than a decade to filter down – in 1970 a greyhound called Black Baby finished a disappointing fifth of six runners at Shelbourne Park. As the 1980s dawned, however, the nation was ready to slip into a state of collective amnesia.

8: THE PEARSE-CUCHULAINN TEN-BOB PIECE

The inaugural meeting in Irish lasted a lightning 21 minutes instead of the customary two hours.

ELEVEN MONTHS AFTER THE END of the Civil War, the rulers of the new Free State were faced with the business of marking the anniversary of the 1916 Rising that had set the ball rolling on the drive for independence. Instead of presenting an opportunity for national celebration, the forthcoming event highlighted the open wound dividing those in power from the Anti-Treaty losers in the Civil War.

The government issued invitations for the official commemorations to the relatives of the executed rebels. Only the widow of Michael Mallen, second-in-command of James Connolly's Citizen Army, accepted. While government ministers led the ceremonies at Arbour Hill, Éamon de Valera led his dissenting faction to the Republican plot at Glasnevin Cemetery. Much the same scene was played out in 1926, with de Valera stealing some of the thunder of the official tenth anniversary commemorations with the foundation of his Fianna Fáil party two weeks earlier.

Firmly installed in power in 1935, de Valera decided to install Oliver Sheppard's 1911 bronze statue of The Dying Cuchulainn in the General Post Office to landmark the epicentre of the Rising. A big row blew up as Fine Gael charged Fianna Fáil with attempting to 'hijack' credit for 1916, not least by rewriting the guest list of the previous decade to exclude Pro-Treaty attendees.

With the rest of the world at war in 1941, the silver jubilee celebrations were quite muted, although some within the government rather optimistically talked up the military parade down O'Connell Street as evidence that Ireland was ready and able to see off any would-be invasion force, be it British or German. A small edition of special coins was minted for presentation to veterans of the Rising, with Taoiseach de Valera receiving the first. A number of commemorative stamps were issued, including a darkly militaristic one known as The Gunman, depicting a Gulliver-sized insurgent armed with a bayoneted rifle standing sentry above a Lilliputian GPO.

The Golden Jubilee in 1966 brought more coins, more stamps and more hijack claims as the State finally felt sufficiently distanced from the events of 1916 to paint the town really red. In some parts, the notion of painting the town was taken literally. As an orgy of pro-Republican and anti-British vandalism swept the land, the residents of Dun Laoghaire in south Dublin woke up one morning to find their shopping streets covered in graffiti. The assortment of republican slogans scrawled around the town centre included Hitler Was A Good Fellow.

As Easter approached and the carnival spirit hotted up, greasy tills rang ceaselessly as the 1916 industry slipped into top gear. Nearly one million commemorative ten-shilling coins were minted by the Royal Mint in London, featuring Pádraig Pearse's profile on one side and an image of Cuchulainn's GPO statue on the flip.

English newspapers that were no friends to Irish nationalism made no qualms about cashing in on the party. *The Daily Telegraph* serialised the Rising exploits of de Valera while *The People* ran a pictorial tribute headlined 'Six Days To Death'. Sticklers for detail pointed out that the British troops featured in *The People*'s souvenir supplement were, in fact, Irish Free State soldiers fighting in the Civil War of 1922–23. And that *The People*'s photo of the Four Courts was actually the Customs House. And that one photograph – captioned 'A rebel leader brandishes his revolver as he cries "To your positions!"' – was in fact from a Michael Collins election rally in 1922.

As Easter Week approached, Kilkee Town Commission voted to make the patriotic gesture of enacting all its business in Irish. One member stormed out protesting: 'I don't know a damned thing you are talking about.' It quickly emerged that he was not alone. The inaugural meeting as *Gaeilge* lasted a lightning 21 minutes instead of the customary two hours.

Perhaps inevitably, despite the passing of a full half-century, there just had to be some re-enactment of the hostilities of the Civil War. It happened, appropriately enough, at the GPO where the presidential viewing stand had been erected for the passing of the Easter Parade. As President de Valera took his seat on the stand the TV cameras captured the fact that there were wide open spaces in the VIP seating around him. Frenzied scenes ensued as prominent persons were shooed in from the margins to fill in the blanks.

In the aftermath, Fine Gael and Labour expressed their disappointment that Fianna Fáil had snubbed them by failing to send out invitations, effectively repeating the hijack claims of 31 years earlier. The relevant government department, Defence, issued an apology saying it 'sincerely regrets this error'.

When the 75th anniversary came around in 1991, with the bloody legacy of 1916 being played out daily on the streets of Northern Ireland, neither of the Civil War sides was in any mood to party.

9: THE CERTIFICATE OF IRISHNESS

All that was required was the ancestral name and the handing over of $57.36.

THE CERTIFICATE OF IRISH HERITAGE was launched in 2010 as an Irish government initiative to provide a form of official recognition by the Irish State to the 70 million people worldwide claiming Irish descent. Applications were invited from individuals born outside the island of Ireland who nevertheless considered themselves Irish.

Each Certificate features the harp and a passage from Article 2 of the Irish Constitution which defines the nation as a community of individuals sharing a common identity rather than the inhabitants of any physical territory. The first Certificate of Irish Heritage was presented posthumously to Joseph Hunter, a New York fireman who lost his life in the 9/11 terrorist attacks on the World Trade Centre. Subsequent framed documents were presented by leading representatives of the Irish State to Britain's former world-record-beating runner Lord Sebastian Coe, Hollywood hunk Tom Cruise and US Presidents Barack Obama and Bill Clinton.

Non-celebrities were invited to purchase their proof of Irishness on the website www.heritagecertificate.com where it was pitched as 'A Must-Have For Anyone With Irish Roots'. Its unique selling points were listed as an 'Official Irish Government confirmation of your Irish roots', a 'Quality product [that] will take pride of place in any home or office' and 'The perfect gift for anyone with Irish heritage'.

The government made plain from the outset that those applying would not be put upon to supply any hard proof of their Irish roots. All that was required was the ancestral name they'd like on the form and the handing over of $57.36 for the simple roll of paper parchment or $172.07 if they'd like it framed.

When the figures were totted for the first 13 months of the scheme in late 2012 Heritage Minister Jimmy Deenihan rejected suggestions that total sales of 1,042 certificates represented a big flop, saying he believed the project still had time to 'gain momentum'.

10: THE PEAT BRIQUETTE

Anyone caught selling coal without the unwanted turf could be jailed for three months.

I**N 1720, TURNING HIS RAPIER WIT** against misrule from London, turbulent priest Jonathan Swift urged the Irish people to 'burn everything from England except her coal'. Two centuries later the Free State government of Éamon de Valera borrowed Swift's line as a slogan for its Economic War with Britain. The standoff, which lasted from 1932 to 1938, arose from de Valera's refusal to reimburse pre-independence British loans, placing him in breach of the terms of the 1921 Anglo-Irish Treaty.

While turf remained the fuel of the rural poor and of the west of Ireland in the 1930s, those living in Dublin and the other towns along the eastern seaboard had been reliant on British supplies of coal from the time of Swift. Apart from the fact that it burned hotter, coal came with an upmarket snob value.

On St Patrick's Day 1936 the newspapers reported 'drastic proposals' intended to curb coal imports from Britain and boost consumption of domestic turf. From now on, all coal dealers would have to register with the government and they would be required by law to offload a set proportion of turf to each measure of coal they sold. Customers would have no choice in the matter. Once registered, each coal merchant would be issued with a certificate which they must 'display prominently in his premises during business hours'. Anyone caught selling coal without a certificate, or without the relevant add-on of unwanted turf, could be jailed for up to three months.

Adverts for Robertson's Patent Peat Machines able to 'procure and press' briquettes at the rate of 60 sods per minute had gone on sale in 1923 and by the 1930s the peat briquette was a familiar sight in shops across Ireland. And yet those tens of thousands of householders who had been burning coal for generations remained convinced that the peat briquette was the poor man's fuel in every sense.

Adverts in 1937 for Shamrock Turf Briquettes played the green card, pitching them as The National Fuel and urging shoppers to 'support Irish manufacture and save money'. The depth of the consumer resistance can be measured in the line: 'A trial of this fuel will convince householders of its economy.' Clearly, very many still refused to be convinced.

That lack of conviction was resolved for the foot-draggers a few short years later when coal supplies from Britain shrank to nothing with the onset of the Second World War, and turf was the only thing that kept the home fires burning – apart from the many tons of wood the populace scavenged by hook or by crook.

In 1943, in response to a crime spree, the authorities appealed to the citizens of Dublin's inner city to report the theft from unoccupied houses of banisters, staircases, doors and entire wooden floors. Trees were disappearing from public parks and streets at an alarming rate.

In the midst of this fuel-fuelled crime wave the Ministry of Supplies ordered new clothing restrictions, putting a limit on skirt widths and pleats and banning external trimmings such as turned-back cuffs. Cattle dealers and bookies were unhappy with the new so-called 'austerity suit' which only had seven pockets. These special-needs professions appealed to the Minister of Supplies for extra pockets to accommodate the large amount of cash they needed to carry. Their request was turned down. The only derogation granted was to Catholic priests who were allowed an extra inside breast pocket on their waistcoat for carrying sacramental Communion wafers.

11: THE UILLEANN PIPES

The Fuehrer was so impressed that he called Goering and Goebbels to his side.

WHEN THE VERY FIRST EDITION of the *Evening Press* hit the streets in 1954, the new paper's most eye-catching headline reported: 'Boy Will Play Uilleann Pipes Hitler Wanted'. The story claimed that in 1936, while taking a break from plotting world domination, the dictator attended The World Dance and Music Festival at the Berlin Sportspalast. Hitler was reportedly enchanted by the playing of a piper from Dublin called Sean Dempsey. According to the newspaper:

> Unlike the other pipers he could not stand while playing – the uilleann pipes are played sitting. But no chair was available when he came on stage. A Nazi stormtrooper got down on his hands and knees to give the Irishman an improved seat and let the show go on without delay. Hitler was in a front seat. The unusual pipes intrigued him and he sent for Mister Dempsey who explained how they were the true original Irish kind and showed how they worked. The Fuehrer was so interested that he called Goering and Goebbels to his side to have a look too. Then came a request. Could Hitler have the pipes? Mister Dempsey laughingly declined. And now they are the property of his son.

The Nazi top brass may have been impressed with the playing, but the instrument itself would have been familiar to them as one of the 70 or so forms of the bagpipe found from Ireland, Scotland, Spain and Sweden in the west to Iran and India thousands of miles to the east. Germany itself has at least four home-grown forms of bagpipe and Hitler's native Austria one more, made from the skin of a male goat.

The origins of the uilleann pipes are very ancient. Depictions of the instrument have been found on Hittite sculptures in modern Turkey dating back to around 1000 BC, while the Emperor Nero was known to pick out a tune on the bagpipes when he wasn't fiddling. While older types of bagpipes required the player to blow into the windbag, the uilleann pipe represents an evolution of the late Middle Ages which allowed for the inflation of the sack with a small set of bellows strapped around the waist and the arm.

The uilleann pipes we know today are less than ancient in two key aspects. The modern pipes, which are pitched in the key of D or E flat, were developed in Philadelphia in the late 19th century by brothers named Taylor who had emigrated from Drogheda. The American version of the pipes were manufactured to project maximum loudness so that they could be heard to best effect in the US music halls of the time.

The name uilleann pipes appears to be an even more recent creation. There is no record of the term before it was apparently dreamed up at the start of the 20th century by the musicologist William Flood, author of the 1911 tome *The Story of the Bagpipe*.

(The most eye-catching front-page headline on the second edition of the *Evening Press* in 1954 was: 'Evening Press An Immediate Success'.)

12: GUINNESS

It was known as 'Guinness's Black Protestant porter', although this didn't curb its popularity with the majority population.

S UCH WAS THE GRIP that Guinness stout once had on the Irish drinker that the brewers never bothered advertising on the domestic front in any meaningful way until the late 1950s. One bar-stool sage told *Time* magazine: 'It would be like advertising potatoes.'

But times and tastes moved on. With imported beers, especially lagers, making inroads into Ireland the company was reluctantly forced to enter the marketing fray. The first ever Irish campaign cost £900 and didn't stretch much beyond the pages of *The Irish Times*. It kicked off in 1959 to mark the 200th anniversary of the brewery's foundation. The slogan was: '200 Years of Guinness – What A Lovely Long Drink.'

The stranglehold that Guinness stout had on the Irish drinks market at the time can be gauged by an issue that briefly arose when the Smithwicks arm of the same company launched Phoenix, a light ale. The ad agency came up with the slogan: 'Phoenix – The Bright Pint.' This was shot down by the Managing Director of Guinness who testily informed the agency that 'pint' was a Guinness word. The slogan was changed to: 'Phoenix – The Bright Beer.'

When it first went on sale in 1759, Ireland's signature drink was originally called Extra Superior Porter. Porter was a form of

dark beer that originated in London in the 18th century. Arthur
Guinness borrowed the idea from the English capital where it
had gained its name because of its popularity with street and river
porters. The father of 21 children, Arthur was a staunch opponent
to the United Irishmen who sought an Irish Republic free from
Britain. As a result his brew was known to generations as 'Guinness's
black Protestant porter', although this didn't curb its popularity
with the majority population.

While the company's very belated first marketing push in 1959
was a success, there was no stopping the march of the fashionable
new lagers. Three decades later, Guinness was once again nervously
eyeing the opposition after stout sales in the key British market
slumped four years running in the late 1970s. So, in the summer of
1979, the company hit back with an airy brew it called Guinness
Light. To loyal stout-slurpers this was an act of heresy. The very name
Guinness Light seemed an admission of weakness. To suggest that
the seasoned stout drinker would even consider drinking a watered-
down brew was tantamount to calling him a sissy. But Guinness had
blown a huge budget on its slightly-less-black-stuff so the company
wasn't going to give up without a fight.

The Sunday World's Pub Spy was dispatched to get an early
reaction to the new arrival. Before he set out, Pub Spy was reminded
that the launch of the new product was of huge importance to
Guinness so that it could almost be said to be in the national interest
if he could report some positive feedback. The best Pub Spy could
manage was a verdict that was candidly critical rather than glowing.
The review ran, warts and all. So, by way of editorial balance, the
newspaper commissioned another hack to do a vox pop on the
streets of Dublin. He returned with slim pickings. He'd only found
two people who weren't openly hostile, and even they were faint in
their praise. So, in desperation, another reporter was sent out in the
hope of striking it third time lucky.

Happily, the third hack came back with the goods, but the
National Union of Journalists chapel at the *Sunday World* raised
concerns that the methods used had not been entirely scientific, and
that the positive spin on Guinness Light must be set aside. The editor
pleaded with the union, but the NUJ said that unscientific reporting
had no place in Irish journalism. At this point senior management
intervened, opening up the appalling vista that Guinness might

withdraw its advertising from the newspaper. The union stood firm – there would be no unscientific stories in the *Sunday World*. To borrow the Guinness Light slogan, they said it couldn't be done.

But ...

When the next edition of the *Sunday World* appeared, the customary glamorous model draped across the front page was this time clad in a figure-hugging t-shirt bearing the legend 'Guinness Light: Light Years Ahead'. It saved the day, but not even two years lay ahead for the light stout whose greatest failing was probably that it was ahead of its time. In 1981 Guinness pulled the plug on the drink the public just wouldn't swallow.

13: HENRY II's PAPAL BULL

Henry used his new conquest to solve a family pickle, gifting Ireland to his youngest son, John.

AS THE CATHOLIC CHURCH in Ireland prepared for the visit of Pope John Paul II in the autumn of 1979, a pastoral letter was read out in churches across the land giving a proud account of the formative links between Ireland and the Papacy stretching back over 1,500 years. However, the history lesson stopped at the Anglo-Norman conquest of Ireland, which, inconveniently, had been endorsed by the Papal Bull of Adrian IV granting overlordship to Henry II.

Adrian IV was, and remains, the only Englishman to be elected to the Papacy, to which he ascended in 1154. The following year he issued the Papal letter or bull *Laudabiliter,* meaning 'laudibly', to the English King Henry II. This Papal permission slip gave Henry the right to stamp his authority on Ireland, and to enforce a series of reforms on a Celtic Church that took an á la carte attitude to the Catholicism of Rome and jealously held on to the proceeds of its church collections rather than follow orders and send them on to the Vatican.

In 1171 Henry arrived at the head of an invading army to ensure that his underling Richard de Clare, better known as Strongbow, didn't attempt to set up an independent power base in Ireland. In 1172, having reined in Strongbow and his Anglo-Norman camp followers, Henry accepted the fealty of the Gaelic kings along the east coast. The following year he summoned the Synod of Cashel to bring the Irish Church into line with English and continental practices.

With the territory around Dublin known as The Pale in his grip, Henry used his new conquest to solve a family problem, gifting it to his youngest son John (later cast as the villain in the Robin Hood sagas) who, as an infant, was stuck with the unflattering nickname John Lackland. In 1177, at the age of ten, John was made Lord of Ireland with Henry claiming he had authority to do so based on the Papal say-so of *Laudabiliter*.

Three centuries later when Henry VIII fell out with the Vatican he did away with the petty business of the Lordship and declared Ireland a fully blown kingdom with him as King.

14: THE DUBLIN TRAM

Souvenir hunters stripped it of everything that wasn't nailed down, and some things that were.

THE FIRST STRETCHES of tramway were laid in the Irish capital in 1871 and trams began running the following year. Within a short time the transport system was largely under the control of the Dublin United Tramways Company (DUTC) owned by the magnate William Martin Murphy. For over half a century the trams provided the dominant form of public transport, with a brief interruption to services during the general strike of 1913, which turned into the Great Dublin Lockout.

The campaign for workers to be allowed join the Irish Transport and General Workers Union was shot down by employers, with Murphy galvanising the resistance of his fellow big employers. Although Ireland was a part of the United Kingdom, Dublin's tram workers were paid a good deal less than their counterparts in Belfast or Liverpool. In addition, staff recruited to Murphy's transport company faced an uncertain probation period of up to six years, while they were liable to a range of punitive fines if any breaches of the regulations were reported by Murphy's network of embedded spies and informers. The Lockout orchestrated by employers broke the strike, and those tram workers admitted back to work returned the poorer for the experience.

The DUTC diversified into bus transport in 1925 and the writing was on the wall for the company's trams. On a Saturday evening in July 1949 the last tram left Nelson's Pillar in the city centre for Dalkey on the southern curve of Dublin Bay. A large crowd turned out to wave off the driver and his two decks full of fellow travellers. There was a great deal of drink taken, both by those on board and amongst the singing, jostling throng that greeted the tram's arrival at the Dalkey terminus.

In addition to the drink, there was much else taken by the revellers. Souvenir hunters stripped the tram of everything that wasn't nailed down, and some things that were. One enthusiastic collector ran off with the front brake lever, so that the final journey of the empty vehicle back to O'Connell Street had to be made ignominiously in reverse.

A week later the Minister for Justice General Seán Mac Eoin faced embarrassing questions in the Dáil chamber about the debacle. He surprised his listeners by suggesting that he'd been half-expecting the riot that developed. He told the House: 'A force of 60 guards, including two superintendents, one inspector, eight sergeants and three motor-cyclists were placed on duty over the route. The crowds were so big, however, that even this force failed to prevent souvenir hunters from damaging the trams ... No person is being charged in connection with the matter.'

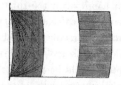

15: THE TRICOLOUR

They returned with a new Irish flag designed by a group of French women.

IN 1848, CONVINCED THAT Daniel O'Connell's campaign for the repeal of the union with Britain was running out of steam, and that The Liberator himself was too embedded with the British Establishment, the leaders of the Young Ireland movement took themselves off to France to witness the revolution that had ignited in Paris and across many of Europe's major cities. Thomas Francis Meagher and William Smith O'Brien returned to Ireland with a new Irish flag designed and presented to them by a group of French women. Just as the revolutionary French tricolour was intended to represent all the people of France, the one of green, white and orange presented to the Irish delegation was to symbolise Ireland's nationalist and unionist traditions with a white comfort zone of peace between them.

The tricolour spent most of the next seven decades in mothballs before it was raised above Dublin's General Post Office during the 1916 Rising. It was subsequently adopted by the new Free State in 1922 and ratified in the 1937 Constitution of Ireland. Before the tricolour became the badge of the 26 Counties, several flags represented the whole island, although nearly all of them were British impositions.

The first official flag of Ireland consisted of three crowns on a blue field with a white border. The flag was designed as the banner of the Lordship of Ireland in 1177 for the ten-year-old Prince John, who would grow up to become the scheming King John of the Robin Hood romances. In 1542, while he set about suppressing the monasteries of Ireland to confiscate their immense wealth, Henry VIII decided to make himself King of Ireland where his predecessors had been happy with the title of Lord. Henry gave Ireland its enduring symbol of the harp, placing it on a field of blue.

After staging a successful revolt against London rule in 1641, the Confederacy of Old English and Gaelic leaders set up their own government and adopted a gold harp against a green background as their flag. Their experiment with Home Rule was crushed with the arrival of Oliver Cromwell in 1649. In 1801 Ireland was incorporated into the United Kingdom and the diagonal red Cross of Saint Patrick was added to the Union Jack which remained the official flag of Ireland until independence in 1922.

While some institutions, such as Trinity College and the Royal Dublin Society, continued to fly the Union Flag beside, or sometimes instead of, the tricolour in the South, the flags issue became a highly emotive touchstone of identity in Northern Ireland from the outset. In April 1954 the Flags & Emblems Act passed into law in the North. The legislation empowered the Royal Ulster Constabulary to remove any flag or emblem from public or private property if the police deemed it likely to cause a breach of the peace. The Union Jack was explicitly exempted from the legislation on the grounds that it could never be considered provocative. Anyone flying the tricolour in a manner that irked the authorities faced five years in jail.

16: IRISH WHISKEY

The Scots, with their superior Irish-designed technology, took advantage to flood the global market.

AFTER THE IRISH POTATO CROP failed in the autumn of 1845, the London-based publishers of *The Spectator* reflected gravely: 'Ireland is threatened with a thing that is read of in history, and in distant countries, but scarcely in our own land and time – a famine. Whole fields of the root have rotted in the ground and many a family sees its sole provision for the year destroyed.'

The Spectator was one of the few English publications to show any concern that Ireland, in the throes of a massive population explosion, was on the brink of disaster. After the following year's crop also came out of the ground blackened with blight, the *London Farmer's Journal* admitted that maybe the Irish hadn't been exaggerating their troubles after all. The solution the *Journal* put forward underlined the fact that there was plenty of food in Ireland for those who could afford it, while recognising that a British administration ideologically committed to unfettered market forces would have to be persuaded that there was something in it for them if they were to help the starving Irish.

To this end the *London Farmer's Journal* called on Prime Minister Sir Robert Peel to ban the use of grain for distilling whiskey in Ireland. This measure, argued the publication, would have the double benefit of freeing up wheat and barley for food, and 'benefit our West Indian colonies by causing the Irish distillers to substitute sugar for malt, barley and oats'.

Peel, a staunch free-marketer, made some strictly tokenistic gestures towards subsidising food for Ireland's poor but was ousted from office within weeks of the *Journal's* suggestion. The whiskey distilleries owned by the ruling class held on jealously to their supplies of malt, barley and oats, but they continued to ignore the virtues of a new and greatly improved type of still patented by Dubliner Aeneas Coffey in 1830.

The Coffey Still produced whiskey with a much higher alcohol-by-volume concentration than the traditional pot still. While the Irish gave the Coffey Still the cold shoulder, the Scots saw its worth and replaced their inefficient old stills. Despite falling behind with the technology, Irish distillers continued to dominate the world's whiskey market until the de Valera government started its Economic War with Britain in 1932. The Free State slapped high tariffs on imports from the UK, and the UK responded with stiff duties on Irish goods. The Scots, with their superior Irish-designed technology took advantage to flood the market not just in Britain, but in North America and India, the world's most populous whiskey-tippling nation.

17: 20 MAJOR CIGARETTES

Even Irishmen who would die for their country refuse to smoke for it.

I N 1964 THE US SURGEON GENERAL finally broke the news that the tobacco industry had lobbied long to suppress: that smoking caused cancer and probably heart disease. The tobacco giants attempted to promote filter-tipped cigarettes as a healthy alternative to non-tipped, but in Ireland, as elsewhere, macho male smokers dismissed filter-tips as girly.

In 1966 P. J. Carroll of Dundalk launched Major as Ireland's first tipped cigarette targeted at real men. Size was important, said the advertising, emphasising the product's manly girth. The slogan was: 'Major breakthrough in big smoking enjoyment.' Health and image conscious male smokers fell for the line, and Major quickly grabbed a remarkable 25 per cent of the entire Irish market.

While all of the tobacco consumed in Ireland today is imported, that was not always the case. There is a claim, which can neither be proven nor disproven, that the first tobacco grown in Europe was planted on the Cork estate of Sir Walter Raleigh. The adventurer who introduced both tobacco and the potato to the Old World was Mayor of the town of Youghal in 1588 and 1589.

Tobacco smoking flourished in Britain and Ireland under the reign of Queen Elizabeth I, but her successor James I condemned it as 'a vile and stinking custom' in his treatse *A Counterblaste To Tobacco*. James didn't ban tobacco cultivation in Ireland, but his grandson Charles II did.

Tobacco growing was once again legalised in Ireland in 1779, shortly after the American Revolution disrupted the supply from Virginia and the other colonies to Britain. Over the following decades the supply of Irish tobacco to the British market boomed, until, with Britain and the United States mending their fences, the Westminster Parliament cut Ireland out of the loop again with a fresh prohibition on cultivation. As the Victorian enthusiast Sir Nugent Everard was fond of remarking, the sole obstacle to growing tobacco in Ireland had everything to do with politics and nothing to do with climate.

In 1898 Colonel Everard persuaded the Westminster government to once again permit the commercial growth of tobacco in Ireland. He turned over a large part of his 300-acre estate at Randalstown, County Meath, to the crop. He also encouraged other landowners in the vicinity to grow tobacco, on the basis that his on-site processing plant had the spare capacity to prepare their output for sale to manufacturers. By the 1920s commercial tobacco planting had generated some 100 jobs in the locality.

However, the Irish tobacco-growing sector faced two major problems, both of which would prove insurmountable. The first was that, in order to survive at all against the economies of scale available to Big Tobacco, the puny Irish operations required a substantial State subsidy, first from Westminster and then from the Free State.

In 1928 the Irish government declared that the industry must either stand or fall on its own feet, in the full knowledge there was going to be only one outcome. Announcing the abolition of the subsidies, the Minister for Agriculture told the Dáil: 'We may as well face the facts. Tobacco cannot be grown in this country to compete in price or quantity with tobacco from outside countries.'

The leader writer of *The Irish Times* was forced reluctantly to agree, pointing out the second fatal flaw in the business model. 'Irish tobacco – however sound, pure and chemically admirable – has failed to commend itself to the modern smoker's taste. Even Irishmen who, perhaps, would die for their country refuse to smoke for it.'

18: THE PENNY COIN

There were rebukes from Britain that the quiz answer breached Irish neutrality.

PRESENTED BY BUNNY CARR, *Quicksilver* was one of the big ratings toppers throughout the first two decades of Irish television. The quiz show was famous for its poor prizes, which started at one old penny, and even poorer answering. For instance ...

> Q: What was Ghandi's first name?
> A: Goosey-Goosey.

> Q: What was Hitler's first name?
> A: Heil!

The eccentric musical clues provided by organist Norman Medcalf have also entered legend. Once, to suggest the answer 'Meath', he played 'Meet Me In Kentucky'.

As a reliable source of hilarity, however, *Quicksilver* would be overhauled by Larry Gogan's 'Just A Minute Quiz' on RTÉ's pop station 2FM. Memorable exchanges include the following:

> Q: Complete the phrase. A little learning is ...?
> A: A lot.

Q: Which fairy-tale character said 'All the better to see you with, my dear'?
A: Was it Bruce Forsythe?

Q: What type of person would wear a tutu?
A: A bishop!

Q: Complete the following phrase. Wine, women and ...
A: Sex.

Q: What 'S' is a native of Liverpool?
A: Scumbag.

Legend has it that the word 'quiz' was concocted by a Dublin theatre manager called Richard Daly in 1791. The story, which has been cited in books and newspapers around the world for almost 200 years, asserts that Daly wagered friends that within 48 hours he could have all of Dublin using a new nonsense word of his invention. The terms of the bet was that the word should have no meaning and couldn't be derived from any known language. The wager made, Daly sent out either his employees or a group of urchins – depending on the source – to scrawl the word QUIZ in chalk on doors, windows and walls throughout the city. The appearance of this mysterious word became the talk of the town, winning Daly the bet and introducing the word 'quiz' to the English language.

While this makes a good origin myth, the tale seems to be as makey-uppy as the word at its heart. The story appears not to have surfaced until 1835, over four decades after Daly's supposed coup. The *London & Paris Observer* and *New York Mirror* were amongst the publications to run it without a source or byline.

There's the additional awkward fact that in 1783, eight years before Daly's supposed feat, a publication rejoicing in the title of *The London Magazine, Or Gentleman's Monthly Intelligencer*, referred to the word 'quiz' as one that was already in circulation. It said: 'A Quiz, in the common acceptance of the word, signifies one who thinks, speaks or acts differently from the rest of the world in general.' The article went on, at considerable length, to assassinate the character of anyone dull or daft enough to be labelled A Quiz.

Much as *Quicksilver*'s Norman Medcalf may have antagonised contestants with his off-pitch clues, there is no recorded incident of any unruly outburst during *Quicksilver*'s long run. The same cannot be said for the equally popular Teilifís Éireann show *Cross Country Quiz*.

In January 1974, under the headline 'Uproar Over Top TV Show', the *Irish Independent* reported that a recording of the quiz at Tipperary town hall 'broke up in confused uproar' after quizmaster Liam Devally declared Wexford the winners by four points while outraged Clare supporters in the audience protested that their team had won by two points. Scuffles in the hall were accompanied by cries of 'Bunglers!' and 'Shame!'

Having escaped with his life, Devally insisted: 'The programme was officially over when the final question was asked. The producer had pressed the buzzer which signals the end of the show but unfortunately neither I nor anybody else in the hall heard it. It was something of a mix-up and there was a lot of discussion after the show.'

Another outbreak of audience argy-bargy interrupted the recording of an episode of RTÉ's popular 1990s school quiz, *Blackboard Jungle*, hosted by Ray D'Arcy, when studio security men had to break up a fight between parents supporting rival schools. The first series of *Blackboard Jungle* had got off to a shaky start, with the producers having difficulty filling all the team vacancies. After it was established as a ratings hit, however, schools clamoured for a place.

The fact that the big prize for the series winners was a new minibus for their school fanned the competitive spirit, to the extent that several contestants were expelled from Series 2 on the grounds that they were 'bangers' who had completed their secondary education one, two or even three years earlier. The rules stated that all contestants must be current pupils.

The biggest rumpus in the history of the Irish quiz show had occurred three decades earlier in 1942 during the darkest days of the Second World War.

The long-running *Question Time* on Raidió Éireann was a national institution. In an era when all broadcasts had to be scripted, and the scripts then vetted by the producers, the show was unique in providing a welcome spot of spontaneity as audience members were allowed to make contributions from the floor.

This small freedom led to a major diplomatic incident when the roving show travelled to Belfast for a live broadcast. Anticipating the answer 'Hans Christian Andersen', the host asked for the name of the world's most famous teller of fairy tales. The contestant's reply of 'Winston Churchill' caused delight in the mainly nationalist audience, but sparked outrage in the Belfast and London administrations fighting the good fight against Hitler. There were questions in the House of Commons, there were rebukes from Britain that the remark breached Irish neutrality, and Raidió Éireann's broadcasters didn't venture north of the border again for a long, long time.

19: LINEN UNDERWEAR

He gave the animal a stern lecture on the Fifth Commandment.

WRITING IN THE REIGN OF Elizabeth I, the traveller Tynes Morrison noted that Ireland in the late 16th century was a manufacturing centre for 'much flax which the inhabitants work into yarn, and export the same in great quantity. And of old they had plenty of linen cloth, as the wild Irish used to wear thirty or forty ells in a shirt, all dyed and gathered, and wrinkled, and washed in saffron, because they never put them off until they were worn out'.

The detail about the saffron was intended as a slight on the hygiene habits of the wild Irish. The suggestion was that the Irish dyed their undergarments in saffron because its yellowish colour was best suited to camouflaging the body's waste products, allowing heavily stained underwear to be worn until it rotted away. Later to be hanged, drawn and quartered for his Catholicism, Edmund Campion travelled Ireland in 1571 in disguise under the name Patrick. In his *Historie of Ireland* published that same year he was pleased to report that the natives had smartened themselves up, writing: 'They have now left their saffron, and learn to wash their shirts four or five times in the year.'

The production of linen waxed and waned in Ireland over the following centuries as its manufacture was banned and unbanned on the whim of the island's British rulers. A flourishing sector in Kerry was wiped out by the large-scale production of English cotton made possible by the Industrial Revolution, but the linen trade in the politically-favoured northeast continued to boom well into the 20th century.

The Old English family at the heart of the Kerry flax plantation came from a line that included the hereditary Pedigree of the White Knight, but no figure in Irish history embodied that association between linen and the colour white better than the Waterford landowner Robert Cook, known to his contemporaries as Linen Cook.

Born around 1646 in Cappoquin, Cook wore only white from head to toe. Every suit, coat, hat, vest and nightshirt had to be white. Cook would not abide any cattle or horses on his land that were not pure white in colour. He was a champion of animal rights centuries before it became fashionable. Once, when a fox was caught attacking his poultry, Cook prevented his servants from killing it. Instead, he gave the animal a stern lecture on the Fifth Commandment (Thou Shalt Not Kill) and sent it on its way.

Unusually for the time, Robert Cook was a vegan. The author of the 1774 book *The Ancient And Present State of Waterford* described him as 'a kind of Pythagorean philosopher, and for many years neither ate fish, flesh, butter etc. nor drank any kind of fermented liquor, nor wore woollen clothes, or any other produce of an animal, but linen'.

Cook's vegetarian diet served him well and he lived to the great age, for the era, of 80. He was interred at a church at Youghal in a white linen shroud.

20: *BUNGALOW BLISS*

At some point Dublin 4 became no longer a physical place but a state of mind.

I N THE MID-1980s the satirical book *Irish Wildlife* profiled the jostling 'types' of a fast-changing Ireland where the old and the new buffeted uncomfortably against one another. In this survey of animal instincts, the sort of person labelled *Taisce Typicalus* would typically have an Irish name consisting mostly of consonants, would pepper its conversation with words like 'dreary', 'authentic' and 'wanton destruction', would eat brunch, drink Earl Grey tea, read An Taisce's newsletter *Heritage* and scour *The Irish Times* for articles by environment writer Frank McDonald.

The sworn enemies of *Taisce Typicalus* (An Taisce being the National Trust of Ireland) included just about all of rural Ireland including *Boggus GAAGA*, *Gombeenus Ruralis* and their offspring *Boyo Redneckus*, who invariably wished to settle down and build a standalone home of his own cheek-by-jowl with his parents on the family farm.

By this point in history, rural Ireland was experiencing a giddy boom. From 1973 membership of the European Economic Community had enriched the farm sector with new export markets and a range of generous subsidies. Best of all were the intervention payments which guaranteed top prices to produce the goods to build up the EEC's Beef and Butter Mountains, Milk Lakes, Gravy Trains and other peculiar additions to the European landscape.

Many farmers building new houses in this era of unparalleled prosperity turned to the off-the-peg designs contained in a book called *Bungalow Bliss* by Jack Fitzsimons. And so too did their sons and daughters who wished to stay local. The country's local authorities gave their blessing to thousands of these individual housing portions which were often built for convenience to face onto the roadways fanning out of towns and villages in a pattern known as 'ribbon development'. To *Taisce Typicalus* and his chums 'ribbon development' was another term for scenery-spoiling urban sprawl in a tacky 'let's play at cowboys' fashion. Jack Fitzsimons' retort was: 'The new generation in the countryside would rather own an American homestead in Ireland than pine for an Irish homestead in America.'

In 1987 Frank McDonald and *The Irish Times* launched a campaign to stop the rot. Cleverly headlined 'Bungalow Blitz', a series of articles attacking planning policy in the west of Ireland posed the question: 'Is it too late to save Connemara?' It quoted one member of An Taisce in County Galway as lamenting: 'The councillors seem to regard us as wreckers, traitors and enemies of the people. Though all of us are from west of the Shannon we're branded West Brits and even as "foreigners" interfering with the right of local people to build where they want.'

The term West Brit was a fair summation of how the speaker and her fellow travellers were regarded by many of their neighbours. Their physical location or postal address didn't actually matter – they were part of a touchy-feely, patronising, patrician postcode of the psyche that had been recently identified as Dublin 4. For decades Dublin 4 had been a leafy, cloistered, well-heeled suburb where intellectuals, professionals and arty-farty types clustered, but at some point in the 1980s it became no longer a physical place but a state of mind.

Rural Ireland responded with outraged indignation. A typical letter to the editor from Galway fumed in defence of Bungalow Bliss: 'Your correspondent asks the question is it too late to save Connemara? The real question may be is it too late to save Frank McDonald? A possible cure might be six months in a draughty thatch cottage complete with half-door, damp walls, rattling windows, an open smoky fire and continuous rain of dust in from the thatch decorating the floors and furniture and flavouring the food and drink.'

But the *Taisce Typicalus* types weren't for turning. They countered that they weren't asking any rural dweller to live in squalor, they were just pointing out that rural children had no divine right to build a standalone dwelling close to their parents and that landowners had no right to destroy the landscape of a country that belonged to all Irish people.

The heated national debate raged throughout the rest of the decade and beyond, and in the end, if it ended at all, both sides claimed the other had won by cheating.

21: THE SKULL OF A BARBARY APE

Despite offerings of honey and meat, it refuses to eat.

FOR WELL OVER 2,000 YEARS scholars and schoolboys studied the *Iliad* and *Odyssey* of Homer, all the time believing that while the ancient Greek accounts of the Trojan War and its aftermath were fantastic works of literature they had little or no basis in real events. That all changed with the birth of scientific archaeology in the 19th century and with it the discovery of the site now accepted as the real Troy in modern Turkey.

The heroic tales of the Táin Bó Cúailnge (Cattle Raid of Cooley) took place the royal fort of Eamhain Macha at the centre of kingly power in Ulster during the first century AD. Modern excavations back up the descriptions, long regarded as pure myth, of the fortification at the centre of the Ulster Cycle of stories featuring Cuchulainn, Deirdre of the Sorrows and the warriors of the Red Branch. These findings suggest that the centre of power in Ulster shifted to Eamhain Macha near modern day Armagh around 900 BC and the kings of the province ruled from there until the site was razed to the ground in AD 331 by a faction from the south enforcing its claim to the High Kingship of Ireland.

One of the most remarkable finds excavated at Eamhain Macha was the skull of a Barbary ape dating to around AD 30, roughly the same period that the young stripling Setanta is said to have taken the name Cuchulainn, in the hinterland of the fort. In his sprawling work *An Irish History of Civilisation*, the academic Don Akenson pictured the arrival of the large primate with the opening lines: 'A special set of palings, stakes five metres high arranged in a circle, surround a special visitor. Even the Uliad's nobles gather close and, like children, peek into the enclosure.'

The ape, scholars agree, had to be a present from one of the Ulster King's trading counterparts in the Mediterranean. Barbary apes were popular as high-prestige gifts in the ancient world, to be kept as pets at royal courts. Sadly, the royal court in the chilly north of Ireland was no proper home for a tropical animal and few would take issue with Akenson when he speculates: 'Despite offerings of honey and meat, it refuses to eat and eventually wastes to a dry carcass.'

Now residing in the British Museum, the Barbary ape buried with ceremony at Eamhain Macha is proof positive that Ireland at the time of Christ, and even beyond the writ the Roman Empire, was fully plugged into a trade and communications network stretching all the way to the Holy Land.

22: THE ELECTRIC LIGHT BULB

A married couple were living in a pigsty attached to a labourer's cottage.

IT IS SAID THAT SUCCESS has many fathers, and experts calculate that more than 20 individuals had a good parental claim over the incandescent light bulb before Thomas Edison patented his version in 1879. By the early part of the 20th century the Irish newspapers were championing electric light as one of the great miracles of the modern age, extending the productive hours of the day, providing a much better environment for sewing and reading, and even acting as 'a new menace to criminals'. The problem was that in the newly independent Ireland of the 1920s there wasn't nearly enough electricity to go around.

The available supply came from a patchwork of small private generating firms scattered up and down the country. The cities and larger towns were generally well serviced by private generators, but in villages and rural areas a lack of competition made electricity prohibitively expensive. Large swathes of the land had no power supply at all, severely limiting the output potential of farms and other manufacturers. The annual consumption per head in the Free State was almost three times lower than in Northern Ireland. Only down-and-out Portugal had a lower per capita energy consumption.

Recently returned from Germany, a brilliant and well-connected young engineer named Thomas McLaughlin persuaded the Free State government to build a power station on the Shannon, defeating a lobby that favoured damming the Liffey. When word reached Britain that the Irish government was in negotiations with German giant Siemens-Schuckert, the *Daily Mail* claimed that a fiendish 'Siemens Syndicate' was plotting to use the scheme as a Trojan Horse to set up a German-controlled state on Britain's back doorstep. First, the Germans would establish an electricity monopoly, with which they would take over Ireland's industry, which they'd then use as a cash cow to repatriate profits into a German economy still struggling to pay back crippling reparations from the First World War. Then, the *Mail* suggested, all hell would break loose across Europe.

Despite the taunts of the British press, the Shannon Electricity Bill passed into law in June 1925. A spot on the river by the sleepy Clare village of Ardnacrusha had been chosen as the site for the hydroelectric dam, the biggest engineering project ever undertaken on the island. In a land where job opportunities were scarce, the opening of this vast State-sponsored construction scheme held out the prospect of steady work and decent money. But when the adverts appeared seeking 3,000 labourers at a rate of 32 shillings for a 50-hour week, there was widespread dismay at the low wages on offer. But before the adverts had even rolled off the presses a huge throng of desperate jobseekers had already descended on the banks of the Shannon.

Apart from paltry pay, the living conditions for many who did secure work on the Shannon Scheme were atrocious. A shanty town sprang up around Ardnacrusha, its population swollen by hundreds of men just hanging around in the hope of a few days' work. In June 1926 a meeting of the Clare County Board of Health heard that between 12 and 14 workers were sheltering in a stable at Blackwater, while a married couple were living in a pigsty attached to a labourer's cottage. On any construction scheme of such a size there were bound to be serious injuries on a daily basis, and very quickly the surrounding hospitals were groaning under the strain.

The pigsty, the stable and the shanty town were shocking images, even in a land of grinding poverty. This was no one's vision of a fresh start in a proudly self-sufficient land of freedom. Within days, the *Irish Independent* had a reporter at the entrance of the infamous pigsty.

The paper reported: 'The latter accommodates a husband, a wife and two children. Some of the places in which men are sleeping are not at all fit for human beings. One place ... was merely an out-office. It might have housed horses or cattle. The beds consisted of old hay, thrown on the floor, with no suggestion of bed clothing. One of the heaps of hay was semi-covered with an old sack. This was the very place in which fifteen men slept up to a short time ago. The number has now dwindled down to eight, and those men are paying rent for the privilege of the accommodation.'

The Minister for Industry & Commerce, Patrick McGilligan, dismissed the reports of squalor as 'inaccurate'. McGilligan had signed the contract tying Siemens to flimsiest health and safety standards. Pressed in the Dáil to demand that the Germans take greater responsibility for their sick and injured, the Minister said it was outrageous to think of asking such a thing.

The nation's giant new generator came on stream in July 1929 when, following a blessing by the Bishop of Killaloe, President Cosgrave threw the switch to open the sluice gates that would bring Ireland into the modern power age.

23: THE HEAD OF OLIVER PLUNKETT

The Lord Lieutenant had no doubt that Plunkett was the victim of a fit-up.

SHORTLY AFTER THE OUTBREAK of the War of Independence in 1919 a cordon of armed republican troops were posted outside the Siena Convent in the town of Drogheda. The soldiers were not there for the protection of the community of Dominican nuns inside, but to guard the head of Oliver Plunkett which the sisterhood had preserved in safekeeping for two centuries. The fear was that the Black and Tans would do to the remains of the Archbishop what the British authorities had done to the living man more than 200 years before.

Oliver Plunkett was born in 1625 into a County Meath Anglo-Irish family of high rank. He was studying for the priesthood in Rome when Cromwell crushed Catholic military resistance in Ireland, and Parliament passed the Act of Settlement. This latest addition to the sporadic enactment of Penal Laws confiscated Catholic lands, barred Papists from political power and even from residing in towns, and banished Catholic priests upon pain of death or transportation to the West Indies.

As Cromwell's life ebbed away, so did the zealous enforcement of the latest set of laws and Plunkett arrived home in 1657 as Archbishop of Armagh. He took to his role as Primate of All Ireland with reforming zeal, establishing new schools to educate both the lay folk and a clergy whom he found to be given to strong drink and 'ignorant in moral theology and controversies'.

The puritan Commonwealth effectively ended with the death of Cromwell (his ineffectual son Richard proved a disaster) but the restoration of the monarchy in 1660 brought another wave of anti-Catholic sentiment as Charles II arrived on the throne married to a Catholic princess while his brother and heir, James, had embraced Catholicism. The Great Fire of London in 1666 was blamed on Jesuit arson, and allegations of a Popish plot to assassinate the King fanned the existing widespread hatred into hysteria.

Plunkett went into hiding, not for the first time, but he was captured in 1679 and charged with plotting to bring an invasion force of 20,000 French troops into Ireland. The Lord Lieutenant of Ireland, the Duke of Ormonde, had no doubt that Plunkett was the victim of a fit-up, branding the prosecution witnesses as 'silly drunken vagabonds ... whom no schoolboy would trust to rob an orchard'.

But Ormonde was not willing to risk his own skin to save Plunkett's, and in 1681 the Archbishop was hanged, drawn and quartered at Tyburn in London, becoming the last Catholic martyr executed in England. Most of his body now rests in Downside Abbey in England, while his head was removed from Drogheda's Siena Convent to the nearby St Peter's Church in 1921, having survived the War of Independence. Oliver Plunkett was consecrated a saint in 1975 and his head, preserved in a glass case, is today one of Drogheda's most popular visitor attractions.

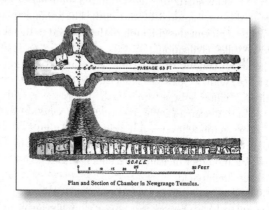

Plan and Section of Chamber in Newgrange Tumulus.

24: DOWTH, KNOWTH & NEWGRANGE

Internal features had been retrofitted in order to 'tune' the chambers as instruments.

THE EXACT PURPOSE BEHIND THE construction of the Boyne Valley passage mounds of Dowth, Knowth and Newgrange has long been a hot topic of scholarly debate, but their status as megalithic masterpieces has never been in dispute. The names provide no clue. The people of modern Ireland know them by their English names; the ancient Celts knew them as Dubadh, Cnodhba and An Uamh Gréine but the language, the culture and the history of the people who built them well over 5,000 years ago has evaporated forever in the mists of time.

When they were constructed to a building timetable that may have taken centuries, the structures sited along the route of the Boyne River served as signals to the gods. With its entrance oriented to catch the sun at the spring and autumn equinoxes – the start of the sowing season and the time for harvest – the mound at Dowth was designed as a great eye in the landscape looking up towards the heavens. Scholars speculate with good reason that Knowth, with its livery of white quartz that dazzled in the sunlight, was designed to signify the sun captured by the earth. The shining sphere was intended to represent the visitation of the sun god to the people of the Boyne Valley civilisation.

The most famous of the three monuments is the one at Newgrange, with its passage and chamber aligned to catch the rays of the winter solstice sun which signals the rebirth of the circle of life. A team of archaeo-acousticians working under the aegis of Princeton University's Engineering Anomalies Research (PEAR) programme used electronic acoustic instruments to study Newgrange and other megalithic chambers in Britain for any sonic secrets they might yield.

The results were intriguing. All of the chambers investigated were found to have a remarkably similar natural primary resonance frequency in the 95–120Hz band, most tightly clustered at 110–112Hz despite variations in the size and shapes of the chambers. The team also found evidence of retrofitting within the chambers, as if internal features had been added in order to 'tune' the spaces as instruments. Indeed, the researchers concluded that the 19-metre chamber at Newgrange (resonating at 110Hz) had been designed and modified to behave as a wind instrument, generating intense sound waves approaching the centre that decreased in amplitude as they moved towards the entrance.

The 110Hz frequency sits in the range of the male baritone singing voice, and combining the possibilities for making eerie music, and the manner in which the midwinter rays were funnelled to light up the stones in the central chamber like living gold, the Princeton team speculated in not so many words that, for the privileged few, the Newgrange end-of-year experience would have been the Stone Age equivalent of a mind-blowing Pink Floyd concert extravaganza.

25: THE STRAP

In one sense it was what might be called an accident.

THE LEATHER STRAP, the rattan cane, the birch cane and sometimes the sawn-off hurley were all instruments used to instil fear, obedience and learning into generations of Irish schoolchildren. Those who supported the practice of corporal punishment argued that once the short sharp shock had been administered the errant pupil could be returned immediately to the learning process, while suspensions from the classroom meant lessons missed.

Opponents of corporal punishment pointed to the potentially dangerous tipping point of the sort brought before Dáil Éireann in 1954. On that occasion the opposition raised the issue of a 14-year-old boy who had been severely punished with a leather strap by a Christian Brother in Dublin's Artane Industrial School. After receiving his first beating, the child was ordered to present his hand for more blows with the edge of the strap. The boy retreated and grabbed a sweeping brush. At this point a second Christian Brother intervened and gave the boy a good hiding, breaking his arm in the process. It was two days before the pupil was taken to hospital where the break was set in plaster, and longer still before his mother, who lived nearby, learned of what had happened. The school's Superior refused to see the mother, and it was only after eight days, and a tearful appeal to her TD, that she was allowed to visit her son. Even with eight days' recovery time, his condition shocked her.

A bullish Minister for Education, Sean Moylan, told the Dáil: 'I would be as much concerned as the Deputy if I thought it was anything other than a very isolated incident, and in one sense what might be called an accident.' Moylan pointed out to his colleagues that there was a financial dimension to the affair, explaining: 'It would be very difficult to improve the conditions under which schools like this operate, certainly without a very substantial subvention from this House for the upkeep of the schools and for the development of what may be essential and necessary there.'

The Education Minister claimed: 'I do not know how the edge of the strap is used, but I will make an inquiry into that.' He repeated: 'This is an isolated incident. It can only happen as an accident.' He also repeated that you only get what you pay for, saying: 'There are conditions that should be created in all these schools, they are deficient in many things; but that will cost a good deal more money from the State than the relatively small amount that is paid now.'

Corporal punishment was abolished in Irish schools in 1982. In 1996 it became a criminal act.

26: THE EUROVISION LOGO

Whether they were shamed into doing the right thing or otherwise, the UK jury voted with a clear conscience.

IN 1993, HAVING STOCKPILED four wins in the Eurovision Song Contest, Ireland as host nation decided to spread the wealth by holding the contest in the little Cork town of Millstreet with a population of just 1,500 people. The small-time location was taken by some Eurovision snobs as a snub to a great institution that routinely attracted international viewing figures in excess of

500 million. One British newspaper went so far as to describe the chosen venue, the equestrian Green Glens Arena, as 'a cowshed'.

The morning after the contest, in which Ireland's Niamh Kavanagh pipped the UK's entrant Jimmy Walsh, the *Guardian's* television critic griped: 'Malta gave it to Ireland with the very last vote. Bastards!'

Perhaps at the heart of the sour grapes lay the long-held belief in Britain that a number of hotly tipped UK entries in the past had been done down by tactical voting. In 1969 there was a widespread sense of injustice in Britain when the infectious 'Boom Bang-A-Bang' sung by Lulu was dragged back into the pack for a four-way tie for first with Spain, France and the Netherlands. However, it was the outcome a year previously in 1968 that really hurt. Co-written by Derry's Phil Coulter and performed by Cliff Richard, 'Congratulations' was so obviously an instant Eurovision classic that it started the evening as the overwhelming favourite. When 'Congratulations' lost out by a single point to the Spaniards, the conspiracy theories went into overdrive, to the extent that fully 30 years later a rumour began circulating that agents of General Franco's fascist regime had somehow rigged the votes.

By the time the 1970 contest came around some members of Team Britain had seemingly formed the view that if you can't beat 'em, join 'em. The early favourite to see off all comers in Amsterdam was Paul McCartney's protégé Mary Hopkin singing 'Knock Knock Who's There'? However, as the big night approached it became clear that the ridiculously catchy Irish entry, 'All Kinds of Everything' sung by Dana, was getting under the skin of everyone exposed to it.

According to the rules of the contest the juries of each country were to be hermetically sealed in a studio capsule while they lent their ears impartially to each of the songs on the night. They weren't to be disturbed until it was their turn to cast their votes in the closing segment. A young promoter from Northern Ireland called Sam Smyth, who would later make his name as a journalist, had been selected to sit on the UK jury. He later recalled that as the Irish entry began to pick up momentum on the scoreboard a BBC organiser popped into the booth and suggested that the jury might consider giving a heap of points to Yugoslavia as a patriotic gesture to derail Dana and propel Mary Hopkin to victory.

Smyth declared himself outraged at the suggested skulduggery. He was joined in his state of highest dudgeon by a fellow jurist who happened to be a lay preacher. Whether they were shamed into doing the right thing or they chose to treat the Yugoslav suggestion with the contempt it deserved, the UK jury voted with a clear conscience. Dana won, Mary Hopkin came second, and Julio Iglesias finished third for Spain.

Ireland's prize for Dana's victory was the honour of hosting the 1971 contest. There was some head-scratching over the choice of the UK's representative at Dublin's Gaiety Theatre. The Troubles had engulfed Northern Ireland in horrific murder and mayhem in 1969. Many saw the Republic's selection in 1970 of Dana, from the largely Nationalist city of Derry, as endorsing or at least echoing a long-held territorial claim on the North. So when Clodagh Rodgers from Ballymena was picked to represent the UK in Dublin the political interpreters went on overtime.

One theory put forward from British sources was that the UK had felt it prudent to send an Irishwoman because they feared a singer from Britain would get a hostile reception from the home crowd on the night. The reverse theory was that the UK had chosen a singer who could be seen as a proud representative of Ulster in order to 'put it up' to the hosts. Given the poisonous atmosphere of the time, no one was too surprised when an anonymous caller threatened to kidnap Rodgers.

Security was upped a notch and the press attention turned to what the singer of 'Jack In The Box' would be wearing on the night. Again, given the laddish culture of the time, no one was too surprised when, after Clodagh posed for the cameras in hot pants, one reporter carped: 'The well-publicised "best legs in showbiz" proved slightly knock-kneed when revealed.' Clodagh's response: 'Well, they're getting a bit fat.' She revealed she'd be wearing a maxi-dress for the show.

In a scenario that would, in the fullness of time, provide the sitcom *Father Ted* with one of its best-loved plotlines, everyone at the cash-strapped national broadcaster was rooting for a respectable mid-table finish. With days to go, one newspaper columnist predicted that, in the unlikely event of a second Irish win in a row: 'RTÉ will express immense delight while it diplomatically offers the running of next year's contest to the runner-up.'

Happily, it didn't come to that. Ireland's Angela Farrell delivered the result RTÉ's top brass was hoping for when the instantly forgettable 'One Day Love' finished 11th behind Monaco's stirring winner 'A Bench, A Tree, A Street' sung by Severine.

27: THE THATCHED COTTAGE

The Land League and their fellow travellers were gifted a huge propaganda tool.

COMMONLY THOUGHT OF AS A picturesque part of the ancient Irish landscape, the thatched cottage is believed by many scholars to date back only 350 years or so when the native Irish – keeping up with the Joneses – began to abandon their round huts of wood, mud or even turf for the new rectangular designs favoured by the English and Scots settlers 'planted' by the Tudors, the Stewarts and the Cromwellians on confiscated lands.

While the picture postcards of the 20th century romanticised the thatched cottage as the heart and hub of contented, carefree peasant living, the reality in the closing decades of the Victorian Age was one of brutal cruelty. With the population of 8 million annihilated by starvation and disease caused by the Great Famine, and countless more scattered around the globe by the collapse of their fragile society, the survivors left behind found that life got slightly easier with more land to go around for cultivation.

In the 20 or so years after the Famine, tenant farmers enjoyed a jump in their standard of living as their output and income increased. Their landlords took advantage by raising rents, but the new prosperity collapsed in the mid-1870s when a combination of bad harvests, a Europe-wide economic slump and cheap food imports from North and South America, Australia and the Ukraine all conspired to drive the Irish peasantry back into desperation and hunger.

When increasing numbers of tenant farmers pleaded an inability to pay rents that had been struck in good times, the landlords enforced their writ with violent evictions. Captured by the new medium of the camera, the image of distraught families weeping and forlorn beside the husks of their demolished cottages circled the world, gifting the agitators of the Land League and their fellow travellers a huge propaganda tool in their bid to dismantle British rule in Ireland.

The two primary aims of the Land League, founded in Mayo in 1879, were stated at the body's inaugural meeting as: 'First, to bring out a reduction of rack-rents. Second ... by obtaining such reforms in the laws relating to land as will enable every tenant to become owner of his holding by paying a fair rent for a limited number of years.'

At the same meeting Charles Stewart Parnell, a reforming landlord who championed Home Rule, was elected President of the Land League. Parnell's political career, and with it the push for Irish self-determination, floundered when he was cast as the villain in a very messy and very public divorce case. The British press gleefully reported his 1880 adultery case as if it were a 1970s West End bedroom farce. Parnell had fathered three children with his lover Kitty O'Shea, whose husband very belatedly filed for divorce.

The *Manchester Guardian* reported the judge's disapproving summing up, which concluded: 'Why the assumption by Mr Parnell of names that did not belong to him – of Fox, Preston, and others? Above all, why, when the husband comes to the door unexpectedly, does Mr Parnell, who is in the drawing-room with Mrs O'Shea, escape by the balcony and fire escape, and then a few minutes afterwards come round and present himself at the door as an ordinary visitor?'

There was no answering that.

28: THE ANGELUS BELL

The simplest approach was a gramophone record but the Archbishop wanted real bells.

RTÉ first broadcast the Angelus bells on the Feast of the Assumption 1950. The idea came from State rather than Church. As the Holy Year of 1950 neared, the Department of Post & Telegraphs decided the national broadcaster should chime in with a contribution to the commemorations. The original proposal was to play a recital of the Angelus prayer but the boss of Raidió Éireann didn't like the spoken-word idea. After negotiations between the Department, Raidió Éireann and Dublin's Archbishop McQuaid, it was decided to 'experiment' with the Angelus bell.

The prayer itself celebrates God becoming flesh when Christ was conceived by the Virgin Mary. The titular angel is Gabriel, who told Mary she was the chosen one. Around 1,000 years ago the prayer grew out of the existing monastic custom of saying three Hail Marys as the evening bells pealed.

As was his custom, Archbishop McQuaid took over the show. The simplest approach was to use a gramophone record for the broadcast of the Angelus, eliminating background noise and ensuring punctuality. Instead, the Archbishop wanted real bells. The only electronically triggered bell that could guarantee good timing was installed in a Franciscan church on Merchant's Quay on the banks of the Liffey. However, McQuaid had no dominion over the Franciscan Order, so he insisted that his own Pro-Cathedral bell be automated. The work meant the original start date was missed.

When the first broadcast belatedly went out, virtually every member of Raidió Éireann's top brass attended the Church and State joint venture.

With the Angelus now a fixture of the radio schedules, Ireland joined the fascist dictatorship of Franco's Spain as one of only two State broadcasters sounding the call to prayer. A publicly funded Italian station broadcast the Pope reciting the Angelus prayer every Sunday. Private and Church-owned radio stations broadcast it in the Mexican city of Monterrey, across the Philippines and in parts of Germany, Canada and the US. Although RTÉ has been criticised for airing what one commentator dubbed 'a bizarre party political broadcast' for Catholicism, the Angelus is observed by several branches of Protestantism.

The arrival of the commercial station TV3 in 1998 caused some within the national broadcaster to call for dropping the 6 p.m. Angelus to prevent the rival teatime news programme getting a 60-second start. There was no ding-dong debate on the issue – management just said 'no'.

29: THE RYANAIR LOGO

The rescue mission to save Ryanair was led by Prime Minister Margaret Thatcher who vetoed BA's veto.

ON 27 MAY 1986 an advert appeared in the Irish newspapers featuring a birthday cake bedecked with a forest of candles. Above the cake was the message 'Happy Birthday Aer Lingus!' The occasion was the 50th anniversary of the first flight by the national carrier from Baldonnel Aerodrome on the outskirts of Dublin to Bristol in England.

But a large slice of the Aer Lingus cake was missing, and underneath was the logo of Ryanair, and the words 'Ireland's New Airline'.

In 2003 Ryanair Chairman David Bonderman wanted to do something special to mark his 60th birthday, so he hired The Rolling Stones to entertain his party guests at the Hard Rock Hotel in Las Vegas. The Stones shared a $4m appearance fee for their 90-minute set, while the Hollywood star Robin Williams picked up a cool million for hosting the event. In the rock 'n' roll pecking order only a Beatle trumps a Stone so for his 70th birthday bash in 2013 the man from Ryanair got in Paul McCartney to run through his party pieces.

It was all a far cry from July 1995 when Ryanair made its maiden flight, which, like Aer Lingus five decades earlier, had consisted of a short hop across the Irish Sea, this time from Waterford to London Gatwick.

For most people at that time the only affordable way to get on or off the island of Ireland was to take the cattle boat to Liverpool or Holyhead and make the gruelling trek to London and beyond by coach or train. In the mid-1980s a return ticket to Paris (£98) or Amsterdam (£95) cost close to a fortnight's wages for most working Irish adults. Founded by former Olympian Tony Ryan, Ryanair had to survive a near-death experience at the hands of Aer Lingus and British Airways who conspired to prevent the newcomer from busting up their hugely profitable stranglehold on the air routes between Britain and Ireland. The busy direct route between Dublin Airport and London Heathrow was one of the busiest and priciest in the world.

In 1986 the party crasher finally got a toehold in Dublin and London (almost) when it began ferrying passengers to and from Luton Airport which lay some 48km outside the British capital. Even then, both Aer Lingus and British Airways tried to veto the arrival of competition via a legal instrument called 'double disapproval'. The rescue mission to save Ryanair was led by British Prime Minister Margaret Thatcher who vetoed BA's veto using EU deregulation regulations.

30: THE IRISH ELK

The largest deer ever known holds a special place in how we have come to understand the world about us.

AMONGST THE MOST POPULAR and imposing exhibits at the Natural History Museum in Dublin are the towering skeletons of Irish Elk with their enormous antlers spanning twice the length of a good-sized human. The creatures were so named because of the vast numbers of their skeletons and antlers found in Irish bogs. Long before they became a scientific curiosity, these remains were used as building materials by the natives, as gateposts, and in one case even as a bridge over a stream in County Tyrone. One story, which may have a kernel of truth, says that the bones of these giant creatures were so plentiful that a bonfire was made of them to celebrate the victory of Dublin's Duke of Wellington at Waterloo in 1815.

So far so good, except that the Irish Elk was not especially Irish and it wasn't even an elk. The first misnomer was exploded in 1746 when a skull and antlers were unearthed in Yorkshire, while subsequent finds have shown that the animals ranged throughout Europe, Siberia and North Africa, with a close cousin found in China. Further studies have established that the Irish Elk is not related to the species classified as elks, although it did have the distinction of being the largest deer species known to exist.

The Irish Elk is thought to have lived from around 400,000 years ago until its disappearance some 7,000 years ago. The Irish remains suggest that it died out here around 11,000 years ago when Ireland was still attached to the continental land mass. While the Irish Elk is distinguished in nature as the largest deer ever to have lived, it also holds a very special place in the history of how we have come to understand the world about us.

A century and a half before Charles Darwin unleashed his stupendous work *On the Origin of Species*, the Irish physician Sir Thomas Molyneux was one of the first scientists to explore the possibility that lines of living things could go extinct. He chose the Irish Elk, which was not to be found anywhere in Ireland any more, as the focus of his studies. In 1697 Molyneux published a treatise with a very long title that began: 'A Discourse Concerning The Large Horns Frequently Found Under Ground In Ireland.' And so on.

The scientists of the early Enlightenment were generally very devout religious men, and Molyneux was no exception. However, it was becoming increasingly apparent that many fossils represented organisms that were not known to survive anywhere on Earth. This obvious fact posed a moral and philosophical conundrum for the God-fearing scientists of the day – why would a perfect God allow any of the creatures in His perfect creation to die out?

Having raised the thorny question Molyneux placed his faith in God over the available facts, writing: 'That no real species of living creatures is so utterly extinct as to be lost entirely out of the World since it was first created, is the opinion of many naturalists; and 'tis grounded on so good a principle of Providence taking care in general of all its animal productions, that it deserves our assent.'

Molyneux's final verdict was that if people looked hard enough they would find colonies of Irish Elk living happily in some part of the Earth. He speculated that the creature had died out in Ireland because of an 'epidemick distemper' caused by 'a certain ill constitution of air'.

With the Irish Elk at the centre of the hottest debate in world science, its fate was taken up by the pioneering French naturalist Georges Cuvier who, by 1812, proved that the anatomy of the creature showed it to be constructed unlike any living animal. So the Irish Elk proved once and for all that extinction did happen.

Which led to the next pressing question tackled by scientists in this Age of Faith: Now that we know the Irish Elk did go extinct, was this because Noah neglected to get a pair of them aboard his Ark?

No, really ...

31: THE PRIMUS STOVE

Every Country House Should Have A Primus Stove.

IN 2003 AN INTREPID GROUP of adventurers from the British Schools Exploring Society set out on a three-month expedition to Antarctica with the goal of following in the footsteps of Kildare-born adventurer Ernest Shackleton. Assuming that the rest of the trek went to plan, the students set themselves the crowning task of locating the explorer's Primus stove with an especially powerful metal detector they had brought along. Sadly, that part of the mission would prove impossible.

The stove in question was one that Shackleton was thought to have left behind during his ill-fated Imperial Trans-Antarctic Expedition which lasted from 1914 to 1917. The Norwegian Roald Amundsen had beaten Captain Robert Scott's team in the race to reach the South Pole in 1911, forcing Shackleton to set himself the new 'first' of crossing the ice-covered continent coast-to-coast via the pole. It didn't go to plan. Shackleton's ship, *Endurance*, was trapped by pack ice and then crushed, leaving 28 men trapped on a barren outcrop called Elephant Island. The Irishman and five others then made a lionhearted 800-mile journey by open boat and returned on a rescue mission that saved the stranded men with no loss of life. Despite the failure of the expedition, Shackleton and his crew were welcomed home as heroes by a Britain in need of heroes as the Great War churned on in a bloody, suffocating stalemate.

The reliance on the Primus stove of Scott, Amundsen, Shackleton and the Arctic explorer Fridtjof Nansen was the sort of endorsement that money couldn't buy. George Mallory had one with him when he disappeared during his attempt to reach the summit of Everest in 1924, and Edmund Hillary brought one when he and Tenzing Norgay became the first to reach the very top of the world in 1953. The greatest thing about the Swedish stove, which was based on a blowtorch, was that even in freezing thin air it could boil a litre of water in around three minutes, where the best of the traditional wick stoves would take up to 25 minutes.

Long before Hillary's triumphant assent just about every country lady and gent had fallen in with the advice of the 1915 Irish newspaper adverts urging that 'Every Country House Should Have A Primus Stove'. By the 1930s it had become an essential fixture of just about every farmhouse, and was to be found in tens of thousands of urban and rural households that lay beyond the patchy coverage of the nation's power grid.

As early as 1910 the Irish newspapers were advertising the devices to the well-heeled 'for motoring, yachting, camping and pic-nics', and when the rest of the population began to catch up during the mini-boom the 1960s the Primus became as much an essential part of a trip to the beach or the mountains as soggy sandwiches, red lemonade and sunburn.

Over 130 years after its invention, it remains a design classic.

32: THE SAINT BRIGID CROSS

A baby was born in a taxi en route to the hospital because the mother couldn't tear herself away from her favourite programme.

BRIGID FIRST WON ATTENTION and acclaim as one of Ireland's most important pagan goddesses, possessing the power to guide the community safely from the darkness of winter into the healing light of springtime. When Christianity arrived in Ireland, the magical powers of the goddess Brigid appear to have been transferred to the saint of the same name who may have been born in County Louth to a father from Lusitania (Portugal) and a mother from Pictish Scotland, or who may never have existed at all.

Christian tradition has it that Saint Brigid wove her original cross as part of a storytelling act, in much the same way as Saint Patrick used the shamrock to explain the concept of the Holy Trinity. One version of the story goes that a pagan chieftain in Kildare was dying and those caring for him sent for Brigid for a parting talk about Christ. The holy woman arrived to find the man in a state of delirium. She perched at his bedside and picked up some of the rushes that were spread on the floor for warmth and to mop up spillages. As she fashioned the reeds into the form of the Christian cross the dying man came back to his senses and asked what she was doing. Brigid used the cross to tell the story of Christ's death and resurrection and the man made a deathbed conversion to the new religion.

Scholars are in no doubt that the reed cross associated with Brigid is far older than the coming of Christianity to Ireland. It is clearly a variation on the ancient pagan Sun Cross, or Wheel Cross, associated with Taranis, the God of Thunder who later became the Greek cyclops Brontes and the Roman god Jupiter. The multitasking Brigid of pre-Christian lore was Ireland's weather deity, while her post-Christian self is said to have changed her bathwater into beer for distinguished visitors.

The Cross of Saint Brigid was chosen as the test card and logo of Teilifís Éireann when the national television service opened on the last evening of 1961. Prior to that opening night the arguments had raged for over a decade as to whether this new element in public life would be a force for Christianity or paganism, and whether it should be allowed to come into existence at all.

Many of those in power in the Irish Republic in 1953 were browned off by a jump in the sale of television sets in advance of the Coronation of Britain's Queen Elizabeth II. Many politicians and civil servants felt that the arrival of television in Ireland would further dilute native Gaelic culture with godless British and American froth. In a radio debate that year a speaker called Eric Boden, styling himself 'a television enthusiast', argued that TV was the way of the future and that while Ireland must bow to the inevitable, it could at least do so on its own terms.

Boden advanced four reasons why the Irish State could and should embrace the new medium as soon as possible. The first was that Ireland needed its own distinctive TV service to counter the 'overspill' signals that set owners were relying on from Britain and Northern Ireland. The second was that, if the State got fully behind it, domestic broadcasts could be up and running inside a year. Thirdly, and this is where Boden's enthusiasm got the better of him, he proposed that in order to provide full national coverage signals could be bounced off designated aircraft constantly circling the Midlands.

Boden's fourth argument, which he hoped might sway a dubious government, was that a national television service could promote the work of the Church and spread the message of Christ.

In 1961, when Official Ireland had finally grasped that the best protection against the seeping cultural imperialism of British

TV was a native service, the Catholic Truth Society launched a final rearguard action against the initiative. One pamphlet argued: 'Whereas people had to go out of their homes to see movies, television can bring all this pagan propaganda into the family circle, with even more disastrous results. This is the big weapon of the anti-Christian forces today. More souls may be taken away from Christ through the gospel of pleasure they absorb through television, than if the anti-Christ would start an open bloody persecution in our country.'

Adding belt to braces, the CTS threw in the following shocking tale: 'A baby was born in a taxi en route to the hospital, instead of in the hospital, because the mother couldn't tear herself away from her favourite programme.'

The members of the Catholic Truth Society may have been somewhat reassured when they saw the schedule for the opening night of Teilifís Éireann. It began with an inaugural speech by President Éamon de Valera who warned viewers that 'like atomic energy', television can 'do irreparable harm' and 'can lead through demoralisation to decadence and disillusion'. The Presidential address was followed by Benediction of the Most Blessed Sacrament by the Catholic Archbishop of Dublin John Charles McQuaid. This was followed by poetry readings from Pádraig Pearse and W. B. Yeats, some song and dance, New Year's Eve scenes live from O'Connell Street, and a closing New Year address from the Catholic Primate of All-Ireland, Cardinal D'Alton.

There were no reports in the next day's papers of any babies born in taxis.

33: THE ARAN JUMPER

Geansaí is a Gaelicisation of Guernsey where the style known as Aran or *báinín* originated.

WHILE THE ARAN JUMPER takes its name from the islands situated just west of Galway Bay, the article's Irish description as a *geansaí* gives away the fact that these woollen garments are part of a shared textile culture that goes right around the coastlines of Ireland and Britain. *Geansaí* is a Gaelicisation of Guernsey, the Channel Island where, tradition has it, the style known as Aran or *báinín* originated.

A significant cottage industry on Guernsey producing knitted jumpers for export to the Continent can be traced back to the 1400s when a royal licence was obtained by the islanders for that purpose. The design of these Channel Island *geansaís* is believed to have spread to the rest of Britain and to Ireland by the 17th century. A traditional Aran jumper is made from *báinín*, which is an undyed cream-coloured yarn made from sheep's wool. The garments were originally made with unwashed wool containing natural sheep lanolin, giving it a water-repellent finish prized by fishermen.

While there are claims that megalithic carvings stretching back thousands of years around the Continent depict Aran-type patterns, and that a figure in the Book of Kells appears to be dressed in a similar garment, the weight of evidence is that Aran knitting was taken up by the women of Ireland's western seaboard not much more than a century ago to clothe their families and earn additional income. The United States provided a ready market for these 'traditional' jumpers with the help of exposure in fashion magazines such as *Vogue*, while the trade got the biggest boost of all at the turn of the 1960s when folk sensations The Clancy Brothers and Tommy Makem wore the *geansaí* as their distinctive uniform on mass-exposure US TV programmes like *The Ed Sullivan Show*.

Prospective purchasers continue to be seduced with the romantic and tragic tale that the garments of each clan are knitted with a distinctive pattern so that family members drowned at sea can be identified even after weeks in the water. Apart from the fact that there is no hard evidence to support this yarn, the pattern-as-identification story seems fatally undermined by the fact that the owner's initials were traditionally sown into the fabric.

34: THE ANGLO-IRISH TREATY OF 1921

Fianna Fáil, among whom there were many well-known golfers, remained aloof.

THE OLDEST JOKE IN IRISH POLITICS asks what's the first item on the agenda with the foundation of any new party? The answer, of course, is 'the split'. The split was part of the DNA of Sinn Féin even before Michael Collins made his impassioned plea to friends and doubters within the party that the imperfect partitionist 1921 Treaty delivered 'the freedom to achieve freedom'.

The tangled issue of how much freedom was enough freedom produced a partition in Sinn Féin that was just as deep and lasting as the one that soon fenced off North from South.

Arthur Griffith founded Sinn Féin in 1905 with the aim of gaining a separate parliament for Ireland. Under Griffith's early leadership the party pushed for an independent Kingdom of Ireland which would manage its own affairs while pledging allegiance to the British monarch. As the younger members of Sinn Féin began to nurture greater expectations, Griffith and his support base were effectively sidelined by the party he had founded.

The next split would plunge Ireland into Civil War. In 1921 a Sinn Féin delegation, with Griffith and Collins on board, signed the Treaty granting a 26-county Free State. Dáil Éireann was, in practice, a Sinn Féin private members' club set up in opposition to Westminster, and when the pro-Treaty faction approved the deal 64 votes to 55, Sinn Féin found itself in the unique position of being both the party of government and the party of opposition.

Party President Éamon de Valera marched his faction out of the Dáil and took up arms against the pro-Treaty members of their own party who had now styled themselves the Provisional Government of the Free State. Pro-Treaty Sinn Féin rebranded themselves as Cumann na nGaedheal (League of the Irish), and won two general elections and a Civil War against their former colleagues. The Treatyites were furious that Dev's faction electioneered as the real Sinn Féin. The Cumann na nGaedheal government made campaigning difficult. Come polling day, 64 of de Valera's 87 candidates were in jail or on the run. In 1926 the Sinn Féin leader de Valera ripped the heart from the party, quitting to found Fianna Fáil in his own image. Fine Gael then formed in 1933 from a merger of Cumann na nGaedheal and two minor right-wing groups, the National Centre Party and the National Guard, popularly known as the Blueshirts.

The infighting wasn't confined to the political elite. As the two halves of Sinn Féin started taking pot shots at each other, a former gunrunner set about suing the IRA over cash owed. In addition to establishing a parallel system of local government, Sinn Féin had also set up a parallel, illegal, legal system. Cutlery manufacturer Sean O'Shea took a case in the Republican District Court for payment of

£226 for arms and ammunition he had supplied prior to the Easter Rising. The Republican judge found in favour of the Republican Army and O'Shea was left to count his losses.

An early attempt to heal the old Sinn Féin split through the medium of sport came after Fianna Fáil finally entered the Dáil in 1927. *The Irish Times* recalled years later: 'Fraternisation, even among old friends, was frowned upon. Some opportunists, in the hope of creating a better social atmosphere, formed a golfing society, and several successful outings were held – but all the Fianna Fáil members, among whom there were many well-known golfers, remained aloof, obviously under instruction from some high quarters. The society has been defunct for many years.'

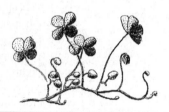

35: THE SHAMROCK

Mary served as a First World War dispatch rider, was painted by Sir John Lavery, became British javelin champion and set a disputed world high-jump record.

ONE OF THE FOUNDATION MYTHS of the Irish nation is that Saint Patrick used the three-leafed shamrock clover to explain the mystery of the Holy Trinity to the pagan natives. However, since the dawn of the scientific age arguments have raged over whether the shamrock of Patrick was clover at all, or the unrelated lookalike wood sorrel. One prominent botanist declared in a paper of 1830 that the three-leaf clover, or any clover for that matter, was not native to Ireland and had only been introduced 200 years earlier in the 17th century.

In 1988 the National Botanic Gardens conducted a nationwide survey to establish just what type of plant the people of Ireland considered to be shamrock. The 1988 investigation duplicated one carried out almost a century earlier in 1893. On both occasions people the length and breadth of the land were asked to send in samples of the plant type they identified as shamrock. The result, by the same landslide in both cases, was that the Irish people of the 1980s and their Victorian ancestors both identified lesser clover and/or white clover as true shamrock.

The shamrock gained international recognition as a symbol of Ireland in the 19th century when it was adopted as the logo of the Ancient Order of Hibernians in the US, added to the flag of Montreal, and incorporated into the insignia of Irish regiments attached to several armies. Glasgow Celtic FC dropped it from their crest in the 1930s in favour of the four-leafed clover, while the Boston Celtics basketball team took it for theirs when the club was founded a decade later. It was, however, as the tailfin logo of Aer Lingus that the shamrock became the hallmark insignia of Ireland.

Aer Lingus added the shamrock to its livery only in 1958 when it began its first regular transatlantic service from Shannon to New York. The national carrier had started life in 1936 with a single aircraft making a daily run from Baldonnel Aerodrome outside Dublin to Bristol in England.

As the new airline expanded, it recruited its first generation of pilots almost entirely from the National Junior Aviation Club run by the Anglo-Irish avatrix Lady Mary Heath who had recently divorced her Tory MP husband Sir James Heath on grounds of cruelty and adultery.

From Knockaderry in Limerick, Mary Heath was a force of nature who stormed through life at such breakneck speed that a headlong collision might always be just around the corner. High drama characterised her life from the age of one when her father bludgeoned her mother to death. He was convicted of murder and declared insane. Leaving school on Dublin's Mespil Road, Mary served as a First World War dispatch rider, had her portrait painted by Sir John Lavery, became British javelin champion, set a disputed world record for the high-jump and became a delegate to the Olympic Council.

As Ireland's most celebrated aviatrix during the Golden Age of Flight, she made world headlines in 1928 as the first pilot of either sex to fly from Cape Town in South Africa to London in an open cockpit plane. She had the world at her feet before a crash at an Ohio airshow left her with horrific career-ending injuries and a steel plate in her skull. She returned to Ireland with her third husband where, during the early 1930s, she would train most of the first Aer Lingus pilots to earn their wings.

When another of her enterprises, Dublin Air Ferries, took a nosedive in 1938, Lady Mary Heath went down with it. Destroyed by a third marriage breakdown, a chronic drink problem and bankruptcy, she died in 1939 after falling down the stairs of a London tram.

36: THE HEDGE SCHOOL

They were turning out Irish Catholics who weren't nearly Catholic enough.

HEDGE SCHOOLS SPRANG INTO BEING in the early 18th century following the enactment of fresh Penal Laws intended to suppress the Catholic religion. One of the key prohibitions stipulated that: 'No person of the Popish religion shall publicly or in private houses teach school, or instruct youth in learning within this realm.'

Native children were offered an education in schools funded by the English overlords, but the off-putting terms and conditions included an indoctrination in Anglican Church teachings and a blanket ban on the Irish language during class time. The fact that there was no great take-up on this offer of State education can be seen from a much later Church of Ireland submission to the Crown in 1825 seeking greater resources. Rehashing an argument that was by then very old, the petition argued: 'Amongst the ways to convert and civilise the Deluded People, the most necessary have always been thought to be that a sufficient number of English Protestant Schools be erected, wherein the Children of the Irish Natives should be instructed in the English Tongue and in the Fundamental Principles of the True Religion.'

The term 'hedge school' is somewhat misleading, as the sodden Irish weather would have made any sustained teaching and learning impossible under the sparse shelter from wind and rain afforded by hedges or trees. It is known that many schools convened in barns, cottages and other structures. There is also little evidence that the pupils or teachers were harassed, or the schools raided, by the authorities. The romantic view that the hedge schools welcomed all comers is also mistaken. Pupils were expected to pay for their tuition, leaving vast numbers of the poorest children effectively barred from education. Despite this exclusivity, the hedge schools remained an important means of transmitting Gaelic learning and culture for more than 100 years. A commission of inquiry report in 1826, when the island's population was approaching 8 million, found that of 550,000 pupils at school in Ireland some 403,000 were enrolled in hedge schools.

In 1831 a new educational system was established in Ireland under a National Board of Education. This progressive arrangement was intended to be multidenominational but the schools were swiftly carved up between the main religious groups. The new regime suited a Catholic Church on the verge of its great mid-century resurgence. Almost as much as the English authorities, the Roman Church regarded Catholic peasant culture, as promoted in the hedge schools, as undisciplined, morally lax and far too steeped in old pagan behaviour to please God.

As the Bishop of Kildare and Leighlin wrote to his clergy in 1831, he and his fellow bishops welcomed 'the rule which requires that all the teachers henceforth to be employed be provided from some Model School, with a certificate of their competency, that will aid us in a work of great difficulty, to wit, that of suppressing hedge schools, and placing youths under the direction of competent teachers, and of those only'.

The hedge schools were turning out Irish Catholics who weren't nearly Catholic enough, and that could no longer be tolerated.

37: THE JOHN HINDE POSTCARD

He would saw down the nearest rhododendron bush to camouflage the blemish.

IN 1955, FOLLOWING A BRIEF SPELL as Fógra Fáilte, the Irish Tourism Association revamped itself as Bord Fáilte in order to capitalise on the new wave of mostly American visitors pouring into Shannon Airport at the onset of a new tourist boom. One of the tourist board's first brochures, *Touring Holidays*, urged visitors: 'Bring your camera too – colour films give better results in Ireland than anywhere else.'

One Englishman who had already decided to act on that premise was John Hinde, born in Somerset of Quaker stock. Towards the end of the Second World War, Hinde joined a circus as a publicity agent where he met his wife Antonia, a trapeze artist. In the mid-1950s they toured Ireland with their own big top, but after two years the show could not go on and Hinde retreated to his earliest enthusiasm as a photographer.

Picturesque postcards of a romanticised Ireland were becoming big business with the swelling tourist numbers. Most at the time were in black and white, which was thought to convey both a touch of class and a suggestion of Ireland's ancient heritage. Hinde struck out in the opposite direction, opting for garish colourised images of sentimental scenes usually involving some combination of cuddly donkeys, fluffy haystacks, rolling hills, swarthy peasants and thatched roofs. And if the scenery wasn't up to scratch, Hinde was ready and willing to give nature a helping hand.

Hinde did some of his best work back in the studio, where he would airbrush out any features that didn't fit in with his chocolate-box visions, and touch up any colours he felt were too flat. He would arrange people and props in theatrical poses, and carried a saw in the boot of his car for surgical interventions. It was said that whenever he was confronted with a feature that didn't fit his ideal image, he would saw down the nearest rhododendron bush and use it to camouflage the blemish, which is why his postcards featured so many rhododendron bushes.

In 1972, with his postcards regarded by millions as representations of the real Ireland, Hinde sold his thriving business to Waterford Glass.

38: THE BUNTÚS CAINTE BOOKLET

They were forced to deny of rumours that they were infiltrating Irish-language Catholic Masses to utter the responses in English.

IN EARLY 1967 THREE SLIM VOLUMES of a new publication entitled *Buntús Cainte* were published by the official Stationery Office. Decorated with chirpy cartoons, these booklets represented an entirely new approach by the State to the teaching of the Irish language. Out went solemn histories of saints and scholars meant to improve the reader, and in came simple phrases which the authors hoped the plain people would sprinkle into their everyday lives. In a further effort to be populist, the booklets were designed to be used in conjunction with a TV show of the same name, presented by two smart young women dressed to kill for the Swinging Sixties, Máire O'Neill and Aileen Geoghegan.

The user-friendly *Buntús Cainte* guide to Irish was rolled out to adults on the telly, and integrated into the classroom with the additional aids of colourful sticky-back cut-out characters that could be moved about a blackboard sheathed with cloth.

The *Buntús Cainte* initiative was widely seen as a fire-fighting response to the foundation two years earlier of the Language Freedom Movement. The LFM formed in an effort to force the State to implement a Fine Gael policy document of 1961 which had pledged to abolish compulsory Irish as a requirement for passing the Intermediate and Leaving Certificates, and for entry to the public service. The strict admissions policy attached to the language excluded a large resentful chunk of the population from further education and permanent, pensionable jobs.

While the LFM's first year was uneventful, its second was to thrust it to the centre of public debate as the State turned 1966 into a year of commemorations for the Golden Jubilee of the 1916 Rising. For many Irish language revivalists the foundation of the LFM was an act of bald treachery, and during Easter Week one group of writers calling themselves *Misneach* (Courage) went on a seven-day hunger strike to demonstrate their commitment to the language. They and their supporters were dismayed in August 1966 when new census figures showed that the number of native Irish speakers had plummeted from 400,000 to just 70,000 in the space of four decades of Irish self-determination.

That same month tempers began to boil when another group of Irish language enthusiasts invaded a meeting of the LFM and overturned the tables while taunting the perceived traitors with a sarcastic rendition of 'God Save The Queen'. The freedom seekers were also forced to issue repeated denials of rumours that they were infiltrating Irish-language Catholic Masses with the vile purpose of uttering the responses in English.

Things came to a head in September, when some 2,000 people packed into an LFM meeting at Dublin's Mansion House. The vast majority of those in the hall were there to disrupt the proceedings, which they did by roaring their heads off, waving Union Jacks, ripping down the tricolour hung as a backdrop to the podium, throwing objects and, finally, letting off a stink bomb that provoked a brawl.

The free-for-all was finally quelled when the people who'd called the meeting and paid for the hire of the Mansion House were forced to open the floor to their sworn enemies, so that every speaker in favour of abolishing compulsory Irish had to be 'balanced' with the airing of the opposite view. One of those on the pro-Irish side who took a conciliatory approach was Father Colman Ó hUallacháin who argued that instead of abandoning the language, a new and improved way must be developed to make it accessible and desirable to the common person. When *Buntús Cainte* arrived the following year the priest was on board as a driving force.

The populist *Buntús Cainte*, which sold an impressive 218,000 copies in its first months, was considerably different in its scope and purpose from the very first Irish language books to roll off a printing press. Commissioned in 1551 by Queen Elizabeth I – who recruited tutors to teach her the language – the first printed Irish books were religious works aimed at converting Ireland's Gaelic-speaking ruling class to Protestantism.

39: THE BOOK OF KELLS

There were power struggles over the date of Easter, and even over hairstyles.

THE BOOK OF KELLS HAS BEEN described as representing the zenith of Western calligraphy and illumination. The book, which dates from around AD 800, was once encased in protective covers encrusted with gold and jewels. The annals tell us that the tome containing the four Gospels of the New Testament was 'wickedly stolen' from the great stone church at Kells in the year 1006 by thieves who were only interested in its valuable casing. The same sources record that the damaged manuscript turned up a few months later when it was found hidden 'under a sod'. The prized covers had been unceremoniously ripped off, together with the opening and closing pages of illuminated vellum.

No one knows for sure whether the Book of Kells was created in Ireland or Britain, or whether it may have passed through the hands of scholars in a number of monasteries at a time when the Irish church was busy reintroducing Christianity to England, Scotland and Wales.

Earlier generations of British schoolchildren were taught that – with the exception of a few early martyrs like St Alban – Christianity really only got going in England with the arrival of St Augustine, who became the first Archbishop of Canterbury in 598.

In fact, Augustine was dispatched from Rome to steer the heathen Anglo-Saxons away from the clutches of Irish missionaries who were making deep inroads into Britain. The advance of the Irish Church, which was on some doctrinal roads that didn't always lead to Rome, had been spreading rapidly for almost half a century. The conversion of Britain had begun very modestly in 563 when Saint Columba, also known as Colm Cille, was exiled from Ireland after falling out with Saint Finian over a prayer book. Their dispute resulted in a bloodbath which left many dead. Columba got the blame and ended up stranded on the tiny island of Iona in the Hebrides with 12 disciples. From there he launched his mission to the Scottish mainland and onward into the north of England.

The Irish Church was warmly received in Britain because it was as much about great profits as great prophets. The hub of this cultural powerhouse was the monastery. The monasteries were a hybrid university and collective farm. The farming side of the operation produced a range of commodities from beef to wheat, from vegetables to beer. They also provided employment for lay labourers, and the guarantee of a square meal in times of sporadic famine. Although Saint Patrick spoke out against slavery, it is likely that the monasteries used slave labour.

But while the farming side made the monasteries self-sufficient, it was the illustrated manuscripts and religious ornaments that generated great wealth on the domestic and export markets. When the Romans withdrew from Western Europe after AD 410, the supply of books dried up, leading the enterprising Irish to go into the publishing business for themselves. The intellectual and creative hub of each monastery was the scriptorium, a chamber where a dozen or so monks would copy, illustrate and embellish.

The spirit of enterprise preached by the Irish monks was not lost on the Scots and English, who rushed to join the Irish-style monasteries which sprang up across Celtic Britain. The monasteries represented a perfect marriage of the spiritual and the commercial. No sooner did a ruler decree that his people had converted to

Christianity, than a demand grew up amongst the aristocracy for the books, ornaments and other flashy status symbols produced by the monks. In time, the Irish-founded British Church would make its own export drive into Continental Europe.

This did not sit well with the Vatican. The native British Church, built on the Irish model, was isolated from and independent of Rome. The Popes demanded a church run by bishops answerable to Rome, not abbots steeped in local politics and infighting. There were power struggles over the calculation of the date of Easter, and even over hairstyles.

It was an unequal contest in which there was only ever going to be one winner, and it was not the Celtic Church, which was written out of English history.

40: THE TITANIC CENTRE, BELFAST

Stead met his end in the most newsworthy fashion he could ever have wished for.

ON 14 APRIL 1912 the RMS *Titanic* hit an iceberg on its maiden voyage across the North Atlantic three days after leaving Queenstown in Cork. The world's biggest ship, which had been built in Belfast, went under in less than three hours, taking with it more than two-thirds of its 2,224 passengers. The survivors were picked up by *Carpathia* which changed course after receiving distress signals sent out by the *Titanic*'s radio crew operating Marconi Company broadcasting equipment.

When the *Carpathia* docked in New York, the tireless Irish-Italian self-publicist Guglielmo Marconi was on hand to board the rescue ship and claim his share of the credit. Two months later Marconi gave evidence at the judicial inquiry into the *Titanic* tragedy, where Britain's Postmaster General sang his praises with the words: 'Those who have been saved, have been saved through one man, Mr Marconi, and his marvellous invention.'

By then he needed all the good publicity he could get, because that same summer endless reports headlined 'The Marconi Scandal' linked his name to an illegal insider trading scam involving shares in his company. His hands were clean, but the future Prime Minister Lloyd George and other senior politicians were caught red handed.

The sensational newspaper coverage of the Marconi scandal was the product of a new type of journalism – entitled The New Journalism – pioneered by the visionary editor William Thomas Stead, whose *Pall Mall Gazette* was a forerunner of the *London Evening Standard*. Stead introduced the first celebrity interviews (starting with his friend, the war hero General George Gordon) and paved the way for a probing new tabloid press. His crusading journalism caused a stir, not least when he raised the issue of child prostitution by 'purchasing' a young girl from her chimneysweep father.

Stead, who had often joked he would meet his end either by hanging or drowning, did so in the most newsworthy fashion he could have wished for. While the sinking of the *Titanic* bolstered the reputation of one media magnate, Marconi, the liner's maiden voyage spelled the end for another, William Stead, who went down with the ship after helping women and children into the lifeboats.

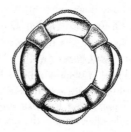

41: THE SACRED HEART LAMP

As in very many things, James Joyce was out of step with most people.

THE IMAGE OF THE SACRED HEART and its associated red lamp loom large in the works of James Joyce, who wasted no opportunity to ridicule the devotion. He wrote of one character in *Dubliners*: 'Her beliefs were not extravagant. She believed steadily in the Sacred Heart as the most generally useful of all Catholic devotions and approved of the sacraments. Her faith was bounded by her kitchen, but, if she was put to it, she could believe also in the banshee and in the Holy Ghost.'

Joyce may have been able to point to the fact that there appears to have been no practice of devotion to the Sacred Heart for the first thousand years of the Catholic Church, and that a wary Vatican took centuries more to give it the stamp of approval, but, as in very many things, the author was out of step with most people living in the land of his birth.

Delayed by the outbreak of the Second World War, the Irish State's great Rural Electrification Scheme due to be launched in 1939 did not get going until 1946. It took fully 20 years to bring electricity to 80 per cent of rural households while many outlying homes had to wait well into the 1970s for a connection. Throughout those decades, workers sent out by the Electricity Supply Board reported back time and again that the first item most householders asked to have wired up was their Sacred Heart lamp. Many had purchased a new electric lamp to replace the oil ones which, in some cases for generations, had perched in front of a portrait of Jesus on the cross baring his heart wounded by a Roman soldier, bathing the image in a warm red glow.

42: THE SOUP BOWL

His leg glided over the edge of the pulpit and hung there till he had finished.

DURING THE GREAT FAMINE of the 1840s, individual Protestant churches and Bible societies set up schools where starving Catholics were fed soup while subjected to religious instruction. The practice aroused great resentment in Catholic communities, where families were faced with a stark choice between going behind God's back and starvation. How widespread the practice actually was remains a matter of debate, with some historians claiming it was relatively rare and that its wicked legend grew with the telling.

Those who 'took the soup' were know derisively as 'soupers' and the practice as 'souperism'. One accusation was that a meat soup was callously and provocatively served on Fridays as this was the day that Catholics were forbidden to eat meat. The Quakers won the long-lasting respect of Ireland's Papists for providing food without the side order of proselytising, while perhaps the most oddball archbishop in Irish history, Richard Whately, also decried the terms and conditions tagged on to feeding the famished as an abomination.

The Anglican Archbishop of Dublin from 1831 to 1863, Whately was the great-great-grandfather of actor Kevin Whately, star of TV's

Inspector Morse, *Peak Practice* and *Lewis*. A brilliant scholar and a noted wit, the archbishop was a pioneer of integrated education in Ireland and donated a great part of his personal fortune to charity. During the Famine, he gave firm instructions to his clergy that they must help the needy, whether Protestant, Catholic or Dissenter.

Whately loved children and was loved back by them. He upset the more puritanical members of his flock by insisting that youngsters should spend the Sabbath enjoying fun and games, rather than yoked to Sunday School desks and Bible studies. Out walking with parishioners on St Stephen's Green he would break loose from the group and clamber up trees to hide objects for his tree-climbing dog to find. He spent days on end studying the behaviour of spiders, but had no time for keeping up with the births, deaths and marriages of his flock, and did not know the names of any of the streets of Dublin where he lived.

The Archbishop suffered from hyperactivity and involuntary movements of his arms and legs. He had a habit of smashing chairs and wearing holes in expensive carpets wherever he visited by rocking violently back and forth. He was also prone to kicking over whatever other items of furniture were in reach. Large crowds would attend his sermons, but not necessarily to hear him preach. He was a hugely entertaining stand-up comic, and no one could ever be sure where his limbs would end up. One witness wrote that the Archbishop 'worked his leg about to such an extent that it glided over the edge of the pulpit and hung there till he had finished'.

Dubliners had mixed feelings about their Archbishop. His hobbies included boomerang-throwing and climbing trees. His cure for a headache was to go out, work up a sweat chopping down a tree, and retire to bed. He objected to wasting money, but the more pious members of his congregation did not entirely approve of seeing him doing the gardening in his second-best holy robes. He was supposed to wear a ceremonial chain, the Order of Saint Patrick, but he couldn't stand pomp so he was always trying to lose it. Once he appeared at the royal court in London without his chain and was told that he would not be allowed in for his audience with King William IV until he'd had it sent over from Dublin – a wait of two weeks.

43: THE BUS STOP

Many retailers now regarded the bus stop as part of the resale value of their premises.

IRELAND'S EARLIEST BUS STOPS were not visible to the naked eye. There were no tall poles to give them away. The best way to spot them was to look for a group of people loitering in a particular area, glancing occasionally at their timepieces, if they had such a thing.

For much of the 20th century the presence of a bus stop boosted property values in the immediate vicinity. In 1929, for instance, a classified sales advertisement for a retail outlet in Bray, County Wicklow, offered a 'Premises. Modern built. Situated in the part of the Main Street close to Royal Hotel and bus stop.' A decade later an advert for a four-bedroomed house in Dublin's Terenure, priced at £1,200, made a major play of the fact it was convenient to a 'bus stop, 3d fare from O'Connell Bridge, 300 yards from the door'. One hotel in County Wicklow even sought to make a virtue of the fact that it was situated only '¾ of a mile from the Dale bus stop'.

Adverts for department stores, jewellers, restaurants and other high-class establishments listed the numbers of any buses that stopped outside, while classifieds seeking domestic servants mentioned a convenient bus service as an added perk of the job.

The trouble with the lack of official markings was that everywhere – and nowhere, if the driver was in a bad mood – was a bus stop. In 1932 one frustrated newspaper correspondent complained of 'thoughtless' passengers commanding the bus driver to stop 'three or even four times' between Howth railway station and the end of the line a half-mile down the road on Howth Head. He bristled that 'on a fine day there is no reason why a healthy person, whether male or female, should not get out' and walk the extra 'two hundred yards' to their destination. He finished:'This sort of thing appears to be general on all the bus routes and undoubtedly it is very tiresome for those travellers travelling against time.'

In the 1940s the government began fixing set locations for bus stops, with poles and painted lines to mark the spot. However, many of these new official-looking stops were merely slapped down where the traditional unmarked boarding spots had been. In many cases these traditional stops were on dangerous bends or impassably narrow stretches of road. One in Dublin was at the topmost point of what the papers described as a 'hump-back bridge'.

But when in the early 1960s Dublin Corporation set about relocating dangerous stops in the capital to promote public safety and a better traffic flow, the authorities discovered that many retailers now regarded the bus stop outside their store as private property, and indeed as part of the resale value of their premises. People queuing for the capital's fleet of tardy buses were a captive market for newspapers, snacks and cigarettes, and no respectable shopkeeper was going to surrender their bus stop without a fight.

The Irish Times reported in 1963 that it was not so long since 'the shopkeepers in Dublin were feared so much by the local authority that the task of selecting bus stop sites, and putting the appropriate markings on the road, was solemnly left to [the bus company] CIÉ, even though it is not the statutory body to appoint stopping places or mark public roads'.

Slamming the politicians for copping out of their civic duties and capitulating to the shopkeepers, the writer complained that:'An irate sweetshop owner, annoyed at having a bus stop moved from outside his door, is to be feared and respected more than the public, inconvenienced and perhaps endangered by its illogical situation.'

The bus company CIÉ did not submit willingly to being handed this poisoned chalice by the local authority and took action – that action being to pass the buck further down the line. That action was raised in the Dáil in May 1967 when Fine Gael's Richie Ryan asked the Justice Minister Brian Lenihan:'Is the Minister aware that CIÉ is issuing letters by the dozen inferring that the entire blame for the transfer or removal of bus stops in Dublin lies on the Garda Síochána?'

The Minister said he would have the matter examined.

44: THE CONDOM

During the 1920s a popular term was 'instruments of race suicide'.

THROUGHOUT THE MIDDLE DECADES of the 20th century having a work banned in Ireland was both a frustrating rite of passage and a proud badge of honour for native writers. Towards the end of his career, the comic novelist Mervin Wall recalled: 'The two words "birth control" never appeared in any newspaper. It was thought indecent even by the editor of a newspaper to mention those two words.'

Wall was not entirely correct, although following the imposition of strict new censorship laws in the late 1920s the term 'birth control' did become an exceedingly rare sight in Irish publications. One of the final references before editors began heavily self-censoring was a Fianna Fáil deputy's condemnation of 'birth control houses', by which he meant the small family homes being built in the new suburbs to rehouse families from the filthy, crumbling, overcrowded tenement blocks. The objection against these small, clean, modern units was that their lack of space for raising large broods of children forced parents into practising unnatural family planning methods.

The other notable mention, carried in *The Irish Times* in 1927 under the headline 'The Riding of Birth Control', concerned allegations of race-fixing against a jockey whose mount, named Birth Control, had performed poorly at a race at Epsom. From the start of the 1930s the term birth control all but vanished from *The Irish Times*, which was considered the most liberal of Ireland's newspapers. In 1945, for instance, there were two mentions, which was double the number for 1939 and 1944 together.

During the 1920s a popular term for condoms amongst religious zealots was 'instruments of race suicide'. The wait for the word 'condom' to feature in an Irish newspaper would go on until 1962, and when it did appear it was once again on the sports pages where – by accident or design – the Waterford hurler Joe Condon appeared in an *Irish Independent* headline as Joe Condom.

Two years later in 1964 the editor of *The Irish Times* finally flaunted convention and used the word 'condom' in its most widely understood sense. It appeared in a review of a new book, *Birth Control and Catholics*, by a member of the Catholic clergy. But this frank use of the word remained very much the exception until members of the Women's Liberation Movement travelled to Belfast in 1971 and returned on the so-called Contraception Train, waving condoms blown up as balloons and daring customs and police to confiscate their contraband.

The civil war over condoms raged throughout the 1970s, with Taoiseach Liam Cosgrave crossing the floor of the Dáil in 1974 to vote down his own government's Bill to legalise the things. His Justice Minister Patrick Cooney told the House that buying condoms 'implies a right to fornicate and in my opinion there is no such natural right'.

In 1979 Health Minister Charles Haughey pushed through his 'Irish solution to an Irish problem', allowing married couples to purchase condoms with a doctor's prescription, and then only for 'bona fide family planning purposes'. Haughey insisted 'this legislation opens no floodgates', which was true in so far as they had already been prised open. By the time of his Act, condoms were available under the counter at hippie markets like the one at Dublin's Dandelion Green and from a dispensing machine at University College Dublin.

But the campus machine was quickly ripped out by college authorities and the strife over condoms raged on into the 1990s. The most extraordinary contribution to the debate appeared in 1991. 'Compiled with eminent medical assistance' and distributed to every Dáil deputy and senator by The Children's Protection Society, it was a pamphlet entitled *67 Reasons Why Condoms Spread AIDS*. One reason given without further explanation was that: 'The more condoms are sold against AIDS, the more AIDS is transmitted.' Another was that, because not a single trader in the County Monaghan town of Carrickmacross sold condoms, the surrounding districts had 'either Europe's lowest, or the world's lowest, AIDS rate, depending on sources'. Without bothering to quote those sources, the pamphlet concluded: 'In a debate, the condom lobby would lose.'

That same year, 1991, the tycoon Richard Branson flew in for a court appearance after gardaí raided his Virgin Megastore on Dublin's quays, seizing condoms being sold over the counter without a pharmacist in attendance. The global publicity generated by Branson's personal appearance exposed Ireland's authorities to international ridicule and forced a rethink, and in 1992 the prohibition was relaxed to allow the sale of condoms, but only over the counter to over-17s. Vending machines were still forbidden.

After the law was relaxed *In Dublin* magazine ran a feature listing the growing number of pubs and nightclubs which had installed condom machines. Days after the magazine appeared, all those on the list were raided. By 1994 condoms were on open sale in chemists, pubs and other outlets, but the publishers of the 01 Area Telephone Directory for the capital refused to list a phone number for the Condom Power contraceptives store in Temple Bar. Instead, the national phone company Telecom Éireann offered to list the store under the name Power Health Products, but the owners declined.

45: THE ROAD TO NOWHERE

The work was so basic that it usually didn't matter what you knew, but who you knew could be vital.

THE LANDSCAPE OF THE WEST OF IRELAND is scarred with haphazard roadways that seem to go this direction or that, as if it doesn't really matter which, before coming to an equally pointless end. These vagrant roads to nowhere were not the product of necessity or enterprise, but of the harsh ideology popular with the Victorian elite known as laissez-faire. This doctrine held that any interference with naked market forces would be an assault on the natural order, and would damage the broader economy and the landlords and traders who drew their wealth from it. The roads to nowhere were the end product of millions of man hours of forced labour inflicted on a peasant workforce already half-starved to death.

Many who considered themselves good Christians amongst the ruling classes regarded the Famine as the response of Divine Providence to the Irish problem of galloping population growth, which left fewer resources for more and more people. The British Prime Minister Sir Robert Peel established a Relief Commission under the control of Sir Charles Trevelyan, First Lord of the Treasury. Under the scheme the Irish Board of Works was to provide paid relief work for the starving masses by forcing them to labour on public works such as laying roads, breaking stones, digging drainage and constructing piers and bridges. It mattered little that the roads often went nowhere. As far as the authorities were concerned, any sort of hand-out simply encouraged the type of idleness and lack of enterprise that had led the Irish into this awful mess of their own making. Relief Committees were set up at parish level, drawn from the landlord, magistrate and Anglican clerical ranks who weren't guaranteed to be sympathetic to the plight of the Papish peasantry.

Getting onto one of these forced labour schemes, however gruelling the work might be, could be a very real matter of life and death. The work was so basic that it usually didn't matter what you knew, but who you knew could be vital. The work foremen would be naturally inclined to pick family and friends ahead of strangers and enemies, irrespective of who had the greatest need for a bowl of soup.

And even if a starving peasant did manage to secure a day's hard labour breaking rocks or digging heavy boggy soil, there was no absolute guarantee of salvation. Early in the year that would go down in infamy as Black '47, following an inquest at Coolcran on Lough Conn, *The Tyrawly Herald; Or Mayo And Sligo Intelligencer* reported: 'The deceased was employed at the public works and on Saturday morning he went to the hill of Gurteens to meet the pay clerk where, in company of other labourers, he remained until night, but no clerk making his appearance. The others went off and he remained behind. Having got quite weak, he requested a girl who was passing to tell his wife to come and meet him, and upon the wife's arriving at the place, she found him dead.

'A verdict of "death from starvation" was returned.'

46: THE YELLOW PACK

The brand didn't survive, but the term entered the language to become part of what we are.

IN OTHER PARTS OF THE WORLD a person using the term 'yellow pack' might have in mind a tricky gaming challenge, a top-class fluorescent marker, an ingenious water filter or even the latest innovation in super-responsive ping pong bats. In other parts of the world the term 'yellow pack' generally equates to something good.

But Ireland is not the rest of the world. Here, yellow pack almost always means something bad. When located in the same sentence as bank jobs, nursing posts, airline, ferry, hotel or any staff, the term is shorthand for low standards and high tensions. Troops in the Irish Army refer (out of earshot of their officers) to the Yellow Packs within their ranks, meaning those recruited after 1994 on contracts that were regarded as inferior. In Ireland's financial world 'Yellow Pack' and 'Examinership Lite' are interchangable terms for a form of cut-price debt restructuring for firms in trouble.

But there was a time, remembered by many, when the Yellow Pack was an actual physical yellow pack. It came in all shapes and sizes, could contain anything from washing powder to cornflakes to orange juice, and was usually stacked in lofty piles that could stretch to the ceiling.

Yellow Pack goods were the first 'own brand' products known to Irish supermarket shoppers – and to everyone else courtesy of heavy rotation radio and TV advertising. Leitrim-born entrepreneur Pat Quinn was credited with giving the term the unique meaning it has in the Irish vernacular. In 1966 Pat opened his first Quinnsworth store in Stillorgan, setting up a rivalry with the country's only existing supermarket enterprise, Superquinn.

While Superquinn boss Feargal Quinn presented himself as a soft-spoken, methodical character, his opposite number made an indelible impression as the brashest motormouth Irish business had ever seen. Having learned the ropes in his family pub-cum-grocers in Leitrim, Pat set off for Canada. There, by day he grew a grocery business, while by night he promoted shows by The Rolling Stones, Beach Boys, Johnny Cash, Roy Orbison and The Supremes.

Ireland had never seen the likes of the first Quinnsworth store when it opened in the late 1960s. It was an age of traditional grocery shops where a large counter with a weighing scales on top stood as an impassable barrier between the paying customer and the carrots, meat, Daz and Omo on the shopkeeper's side. No one got to squeeze the tomatoes or smell the rashers for quality or freshness. After a lot of pointing and wrapping, the cash would be deposited in a wooden pull-out drawer that passed for the till.

Pat Quinn did away with all that, so that the Saturday shop at Quinnsworth resembled a trip to the circus. Perched in a booth overlooking his maze of aisles like a demented motorsport commentator, Quinn barked out news of special offers and great cash giveaways over the speaker system. With some refinements, Pat Quinn's 'pile 'em high, sell 'em cheap' model survived and thrived in Ireland. Quinnsworth and its Yellow Pack brand did not. But the term has entered the language to become part of what we are.

47: THE LEAVING CERTIFICATE

'I have resided in Ireland for years and have heard no Irish spoken in the streets.'

I N LATE 1924 THE FREE STATE government unveiled its plans to provide an Irish-style education system for an Irish people. First, there would from now on be three classes of secondary school. Class A establishments would be: 'Schools in which all the teaching is done through the medium of Irish.' Class B would be: 'Bilingual schools in which Irish is taught to all pupils'. And as for Class C – well, that was whatever was left over.

For those who could afford to stay on, the end goal of the new system was the Leaving Certificate. The secondary school curriculum departed little from the old one under British rule, with the notable exception that from now on anyone answering a paper through the medium of Irish would earn a 10 per cent bonus. Maths through Irish, for reasons that were obvious, attracted only 5 per cent extra. Irish through Irish, and English through Irish attracted no bonus for reasons that were even more obvious.

In an era when many children didn't complete even their primary education, the vast majority of secondary students left before the Leaving. This was underlined by the big box adverts taken out by many top schools to showcase their academic excellence. When the Leaving results were released in 1929, Cork's Rockwell College proudly announced that 33 of 34 students had passed.

Eight of Blackrock College's nine entrants got honours, although the fact that 22 of their pupils had passed the Matriculation exams for college suggests that in some elevated circles the Leaving was regarded very much as a second-class ticket.

Throughout the Protestant community there was, from the outset, a gnawing suspicion that the Leaving Cert was part of an open conspiracy to relegate them to second-class citizenry. This belief was raised openly in 1937 by the headmaster of the King's Hospital School in Dublin. In a polite but pointed speech he noted that of 120 pupils who had entered the Synod Scripture exam, 120 passed. But of the nine doing the Leaving two had failed. The sore Head remarked that if one of those failed pupils had done his Leaving through Irish, he would have passed with honours.

The Principal continued: 'I admit it is annoying to see a boy losing the examination through failure in one subject. Some may look back and sigh for the good old days when Irish was not compulsory.' He didn't blame Protestant pupils for 'failing to warm to a compulsory unfamiliar tongue', but he did blame Protestant parents harbouring 'long and bitter memories' of Ireland's bloody exit from the UK for 'inflicting' their 'prejudices' against the new regime on their children. At the same time, however, he was saddened that the system made it 'almost impossible' for Protestant pupils to win State scholarships as the bonus marks given for answering in Irish were too high.

Happily, some institutions were ready, willing and able to give Protestant youngsters an even break. The headmaster reported that his pupils had secured six of the top places in the annual Bank of Ireland admission exams.

At the end of the same year, 1937, the Church of Ireland Bishop of Cashel and Emly pointed out that in two public examinations, pupils of Waterford's Bishop Foy Endowed School had scored a 100 per cent pass rate. In a third, the school's perfect record had been halved to 50 per cent.

This opened the way for local headmaster J. E. Lloyd Lewis to take the gloves off. He thundered: 'We regard the education of our children as far more important than the acquisition of a smattering of a language which is forgotten as soon as the school doors close at the end of the term.' He continued: 'By Irish speakers I do not mean people able to translate the curious language which appears on the forms issued by any government department. I have resided in Ireland for 15 years and have heard no Irish spoken in the streets.'

Employing a stereotype of the day, he argued: 'The Australian aborigines have their own language but they are still reported as being in the Stone Age. We are not quite as bad as that, but we are on the road to illiteracy.'

His impassioned attack on compulsory Irish was afforded 'a cordial vote of thanks' by all present.

48: THE HIGH NELLY

They ran alongside with shouts of delight and exclamations in Irish, so long as they could keep up.

I N ONE OF THE MOST SHOCKING revelations in all of Irish detective fiction, the florid Sergeant Pluck confides to the narrator of Flann O'Brien's *The Third Policeman* that 'the Atomic Theory is at work in this parish'. The officer continues: 'The half of the people are suffering from it. It is worse than the smallpox.'

Elaborating on how the transfer of atoms from humans to bicycles and vice versa has turned the elderly parishioner Michael Gilhaney into 'nearly half-a-bicycle', Sergeant Pluck explains: 'He has spent no less than 35 years riding his bicycle over the rocky roadsteads and up and down the hills and into the deep ditches when the road goes astray in the strain of winter. He is always going to a particular destination or other on his bicycle at every hour of the day or coming back from there at every other hour. If it wasn't that his bicycle was stolen every Monday he would be sure to be more than half-way now.'

Arguably the greatest bicycle-related novel ever written, *The Third Policeman* was completed in 1940 at a time when Irish society ran on two wheels. The bicycle would become even more embedded in the DNA of the average Irish person over the years that followed as wartime fuel shortages brought car and rail transport almost to a standstill.

The most iconic mount of the golden age of the bicycle in Ireland was the trusty High Nelly, solid and durable enough to withstand years of pounding on the roughest rural dirt tracks. The most famous High Nelly was the one used by rebel leader Michael Collins to get around Dublin during the War of Independence. He'd had it custom-made with twin crossbars in 1919 from the British manufacturer Rudge-Whitworth.

During the first half of the 20th century, Irish cyclists were well served by a large domestic manufacturing, maintenance and repair sector. Raleigh Bicycles rolled out of a franchised factory in central Dublin, while Brown Thomas competed at the value end of the market, selling bikes for £3-7-6 cash or six shillings a month hire purchase.

But Ireland's love affair with the bicycle had got off to a rocky start. Historian Brian Griffin has related how one alarmed rural dweller reacted to his first sight of a cyclist by hurling stones at the strange fast-moving contraption. Griffin quoted a diary entry from one of three cyclists approaching the Galway village of Spiddal in the 1880s which foreshadowed a scene from the movie *Close Encounters of The Third Kind*. As darkness began to fall the intrepid trio switched on their lamps. According to the diary:

> It happened to be a Roman Catholic holiday and, as is customary in that district, the people had assembled in crowds at every convenient place along the roadside to chat or indulge in rustic games. As we noiselessly approached every voice grew silent and they gazed, awestruck, at the mysterious light now seen clear against the murky sky – as we gained the top of one of those sharp, stiff hills which follow each other in rapid succession on that mountain road ... But as soon as we had passed, and they saw that we were real flesh and blood, and not a visitation of the Evil

One, or a Will-o'-The-Wisp taking a constitutional along the high road, they ran alongside with shouts of delight and exclamations in Irish, so long as they could keep up.

By the turn of the 20th century, the craze had swept Ireland as both an adventure sport and a practical means of getting from A to B, while greater availability and falling prices were fast turning the Irish into a nation of bicycle owners. In 1898 the publication *Irish Tourist* ran a piece entitled 'Dublin Fifty Years Hence' which imagined that the River Liffey from Capel Street to the Custom House would be pumped dry to create a long, broad cycleway. Fifty years on the Liffey still flowed uninterrupted to the sea, but the vision of Dublin as a city of bicycles had otherwise come true. Indeed, six years later in 1954 it was even called just that in a newspaper article headed 'Are You A Road Menace?'

The question was not directed only at motorists. The writer argued: 'Cars are not the only offenders. What of the bicycle menace? Dublin alone, sometimes known as The City of The Bicycles, offers some startling lapses of road safety. Defective brakes, lack of rear lights, cycling three abreast, swerving unexpectedly, taking chances in crowded traffic – all play their part in the toll of road accidents.'

Fifteen years further on, as mud-slinging in the advance of the 1969 general election reached slapstick levels, the image of cycling hit a pre-Lance Armstrong all-time low, as Fianna Fáil's whimsical Justice Minister Micheal O'Morain attacked Fine Gael for being soft on crime. O'Morain insisted the opposition party was failing to protect the law-abiding public from 'the thug, the robber, the flick-knife operator and the gentlemen in Dublin with their bicycle chains'. The insinuation that Dubliners were given to brandishing bicycle chains as deadly weapons drew angry protests from the peaceable citizens of the capital.

Betraying a preoccupation with bicycles worthy of Flann O'Brien's Sergeant Pluck, the Minister from Mayo continued: 'The Fine Gael spokesmen evidently are unaware of the fact that modern criminals are equipped with fast cars, two-way radios and are on planes out of the country within hours of serious robberies if they are not apprehended. Fine Gael would have the gardaí chasing these gentlemen on punctured bicycles.'

49: THE BORDER CUSTOMS POST

Southerners were travelling North to post their letters, saving a halfpenny on the price of every stamp.

O N THE FIRST DAY OF APRIL 1923 the partition of Ireland became a concrete reality, in a step that many on both sides of the new border would have wished to dismiss as a bad April Fools' Day joke.

The Free State had come into being the previous December, but the dividing line between north and south had remained largely imaginary. It came as a bolt from the blue to many, Nationalist and Unionist alike, when the Southern government began hurried preparations in March 1923 to make the border real.

In late March the Free State published a list of 'approved' cross-border roads which would now be manned with customs checkpoints. In order to raise revenues and protect local manufacturers, the cash-strapped Irish government published a long list of goods that would be subject to stiff new import duties from April. Southern consumers were horrified to learn they'd be paying a lot more for tobacco, cigarettes, beer, wine, spirits, perfumes, sugar, chocolate, playing cards, matches, cars, motorbikes, clocks, watches, gramophones and many more of life's luxuries.

The importation of some goods was banned outright, with warnings of 'severe penalties' for anyone caught bringing in extracts of tea, coffee, chicory or tobacco. Other prohibited imports included dogs, guns, foreign editions of books and music, cocaine and heroin. Recognising that rural folk living close to the border were likely simply to ignore its existence, the new legislation allowed that farm produce could move freely north and south untaxed 'by any road, approved or not'. Meanwhile, the ports linking Ireland and Britain were fitted out for baggage searches of passengers moving in both directions who would now be classified as 'foreign' travellers. The shopkeepers of Dundalk, Drogheda and Dublin wailed that they would be ruined by the new tariffs, to no avail. The IRA, meanwhile, blew up one of the newly erected customs huts at Emyvale in Monaghan.

The general public responded in a manner which would be repeated time and again into the 21st century. Thousands made a beeline for the North on a mission to shop till they dropped. In the last days of March stores in the North were swamped with day trippers, including many southern shop owners, who cleaned out supplies of goods that were more readily available in the North than the South. One report stated that Donegal's shopkeepers had laid in a two-month stockpile of cheap goods to sell on at a profit.

In the final 48 hours of March 1923, the rush to beat the deadline became a frenzy. One report said that in the race against time involving 'the tobacco dealers, the jam manufacturers, the match makers and vendors of 101 articles … the importers won'. The race went right down to the line. The articles earmarked to attract the biggest single chunk of duty were cars and motorbikes, and there was a mad last-minute dash to get them into the Free State before the customs barriers went up. Many of those hoping to bring in a new vehicle hopped on the steam-packet passenger boats to Liverpool and Holyhead with their chequebooks.

One newspaper reported: 'The carrying companies rose to the occasion and … when the last of the London and North-Western boats steamed from Holyhead at 3.30 a.m. there was not a motor car, a motor bicycle or a pedal bicycle [left in the docks area].' Such was the volume of vehicles and other goods that crossed Irish Sea in the last days that the small port of Greenore in County Louth was kept busy handling the overflow of traffic.

Not all the importers were as smart as they'd liked to think. Some were left with hundreds of pushbikes on their hands, having imported them in the mistaken belief that they would attract the new import duties.

In the first days of April 1923 the price of five Woodbine cigarettes soared by threepence in the South. Within a short space of time the cost of living South of the border was much higher than in the North to the point that people were even travelling North to post their letters, saving a halfpenny on the price of every stamp.

Prohibition in the US was into its fourth year, and the booze-smuggling industry was well on its way to creating an empire of organised crime there. In Ireland, a similar cross-border smuggling business would quickly follow suit. However, the first prosecution for smuggling in the Free State didn't involve either the land border or even someone Irish. Six weeks into the new regime a German sea captain and his ship's cook were given hefty fines of £25 and £9 respectively for attempting to smuggle in 18 German watches, 500 cigars, a bag of tobacco and an alarm clock.

The captain pleaded that he'd bought the 18 watches for his wife back in Hamburg. The judge did not believe him.

50: THE 45-RPM HUCKLEBUCK

In this perverse parallel universe the test of a good self-penned number was that the audience wouldn't recognise it as such.

THE GOLDEN AGE OF THE IRISH SHOWBAND spanned less than 15 years, from the late 1950s to, at a stretch, the very early 1970s. The number of great records to come out of the entire era could be as high as two, if you include Joe Dolan's 1969 international smash 'Make Me An Island'. The lone disc indisputably worthy of the accolade 'great' is 'The Hucklebuck' by Brendan Boyer & The Royal Showband. The single topped the Irish charts for seven weeks in 1965, three years after The Beatles had supported Ireland's Elvis at the Liverpool Empire Theatre.

'The Hucklebuck' had been around for yonks when the big-lunged Boyer cut the definitive version. Chuck Berry had taken it into the Billboard charts in 1960 as a counterpart to Chubby Checker's uncannily similar smash 'The Twist'. The song had first been a hit for its writer Paul Williams in 1949 when the risqué dance it spawned outraged the parents of Middle America before the term 'teenager' had even been coined.

By the mid-1960s Ireland's teenagers were ready at last for some dirty dancing, which largely accounts for the electric impact Boyer's revved-up rendition had on the heaving ballrooms of romance. There was even enough positive charge left over (just about) to propel him back to the top of the charts a few months later with the foot-weary 'Don't Lose Your Hucklebuck Shoes'.

There are several good reasons why a showband scene that flourished for so long produced virtually no half-decent vinyl. For one thing, the recording facilities in Ireland would have embarrassed Thomas Edison, prompting Jim Tobin of The Firehouse Showband to lament: 'My voice comes out very flat on tape, but singing's a lot better than shovelling gravel for a living.'

There was the additional fact that the showbands knew their place. They were well paid to be human jukeboxes faithfully reproducing the hits of the day from Britain and America. In order to keep up with the ever-changing hit parade, the bands had to rehearse new material on virtually a daily basis. The bigger outfits fitted special record players, with sprung suspension, into their coaches so they could listen and learn as they travelled the rocky highways and byways. Lower down the food chain the musicians would have to content themselves with listening in to the Radio Luxembourg Top 20 on Sunday nights in the hope of catching the gist of the new entries. The bands would take Mondays off, briefly rehearse the new songs during the day on Tuesdays, and unveil them Tuesday nights.

One of the biggest bands, The Capital, went so far as to put together a tribute set called The Parade of the Showbands, which involved them playing cover versions of their Irish rivals doing cover versions of international hits. Sometimes, for a bit of diversion, bands would slip in a song they'd written themselves. In the perverse parallel universe of the showbands the test of a good self-penned number was that the audience wouldn't recognise it as such.

The showbands were raking it in on the doors playing other people's songs to live audiences. In the context, their managers weren't going to throw away hard cash on such frivolities as the recording of original material. They would find the funds to make a record when it was deemed necessary, but very rarely if ever with the aim of racking up sales. The main purpose of a showband disc was to secure radio plays as a promotional device for the live shows.

Just how low records ranked in the showband scheme of things can be gauged by an episode involving one of the circuit's aforementioned top acts: The Capital returned to Ireland having recorded several tracks in New York of a very high sound quality which were intended for release as singles. However, when they got to customs at Dublin Airport the officials demanded import duties on the masters. Faced with the choice between paying the tax or scrapping the planned singles, the manager opted to keep the money.

51: THE TARA BROOCH

The brooch was a spectacular rebuttal of racial Victorian beliefs that Irish culture was brutal and backward.

THE TARA BROOCH HAS NOTHING to do with the historic Royal Hill of Tara and probably spent little or no time buried on the strand at Bettystown, County Meath, where it reportedly turned up in August 1850. Manufactured around AD 700, the brooch of white brass was embellished with highly sophisticated decorations of gold, silver, amber, copper and glass in a pattern known as Celtic Knotwork, although some of the priceless ornamental features went missing as it passed through several sets of sticky fingers before ending up in the National Museum in 1872.

In 1850 a peasant woman and her two sons presented the brooch as treasure trove, claiming that they had found it buried in a box in the sand at Bettystown. Many doubters formed the belief that the ornament had been found on private land further inland, and that with the seashore a commonage, the story had been concocted to protect the finders against claims from the land's owner.

The brooch passed from a dealer to a Dublin jeweller who named it the Tara Brooch to cash in on the current fashion for Celtic Revival jewellery. Led by figures like Sir Walter Scott of *Ivanhoe* fame, and the writer of the romanticised *Moore's Melodies*, Thomas Moore, the Celtic Revival movement sought to rehabilitate the pre-Anglo-Saxon cultures of the British Isles.

Together with the Ardagh Chalice, found just three years earlier, the Tara Brooch was a spectacular rebuttal of racial Victorian beliefs that Irish culture was brutal and backward, and it fuelled a surge in national self-confidence which in turn would energise the charge towards Home Rule in the coming decades.

The Ardagh Chalice was held up alongside the Tara Brooch as a supreme achievement of early Irish art. The two-handled silver cup, embellished with gold, gilt bronze, brass, lead pewter and enamel, was assembled from 354 separate pieces. It is likely that the Ardagh Chalice had as little to do with Ardagh as the Tara Brooch had with Tara. It just happened to be found in 1847 in a potato field near the Limerick village of that name. In 1980 another chalice was discovered, this time larger and with a tray and silver stand intact, on the old monastic site of Derrynaflan in County Tipperary. The finders, Michael Webb from Clonmel and his son Michael Jnr, had located their find using a metal detector. As a direct result, in an effort to protect archaeological sites, a law was passed in 1987 outlawing the use of metal detectors for treasure hunts.

52: MISTER TAYTO

Senior executives from the planet's biggest crisp companies flocked to Murphy's door.

ONE OF THE MOST UNLIKELY ICONS of modern Irish culture is an oddly shaped yellow fellow who has been the public face of Tayto Crisps for decades. In more recent times Mr Tayto made the leap from decorating crisp packets to becoming a best-selling, ghostwritten author. At Christmas 2009 his autobiography topped Ireland's sales lists, beating off all-comers including *The Guinness Book of Records*.

The following year Mr Tayto became the mascot for a new theme park outside Ashbourne in County Meath which confounded the naysayers by quickly growing into one of the country's top visitor attractions. In the normal course of events, an adventure park commemorating potato crisps might seem a mite excessive, but Tayto is no ordinary snack in a pack. On the contrary, the Tayto potato crisp is considered by connoisseurs of confectionary to be one of Ireland's great gifts to the world.

The mastermind behind Tayto was Dubliner Joe 'Spud' Murphy. At the age of 20 during the Second World War, Murphy spotted that there was no Ribena blackcurrant drink available in Ireland. He somehow got his hands on a supply and took his first step to becoming one of Ireland's richest men.

The first potato chips sold commercially appeared in the United States around 1908. They came in boxes and tins and quickly went stale. The first crisp packets, also from the US, were made of wax paper sheets stapled into the shape of a bag. Crisps as we know them today were invented around 1920 by Smiths Crisps of London. They came in one flavour – potato. The firm's founder Frank Smith's solution to this uniform blandness was to package a paper twist of salt with his slivers of potato in the bag. Salt-your-own crisps were an evolutionary breakthrough and the idea quickly swept the world.

An avid crisp cruncher, Joe Murphy felt that while Frank Smith's self-sprinkling packet was an advance, it was still just a halfway house, and there was still ample room for improvement. He identified that crucial next step and came up with the simple but inspired idea of making a crisp that popped out of the pack already flavoured.

In 1954 Murphy registered the Tayto company and set his star employee Seamus Burke the task of inventing the world's first flavoured potato crisp. Working on a kitchen table, Burke came up with cheese and onion. Murphy started production of Tayto Cheese & Onion in Dublin with one van and eight employees, persuading the Findlater chain of upmarket stores to stock his new product. Tayto Cheese & Onion Crisps were an overnight sensation, not just in Ireland but around the world. Senior executives from the planet's biggest crisp companies flocked to Murphy's door to buy a piece of the action.

Murphy poured his new-found wealth back into marketing the company. Tayto's sponsored radio programmes like *Cruising With Tayto and Leisure Time* ('Take it easy with Tayto') became staples of the schedules. Tayto neon signs became part of the urban landscape. School rulers stamped with the Tayto logo circulated in classrooms.

More than six decades on, the Irish were munching through an average three packets of crisps each week, most of them Tayto.

53: AN FÁINNE NUA

Opposition to the restoration of the language should be made a matter of treason.

THE PRESERVATION OF THE Irish language has divided opinion in Ireland since long before the foundation of the independent state. Daniel O'Connell famously said of it: 'I am sufficiently utilitarian not to regret its abandonment.' The Liberator believed that for his people to take their place among the nations of the world, they must liberate themselves from a language of the dispossessed.

Almost a century later, having been dealt a mortal blow by the Great Famine, the language was being maintained on life support by the coming men of Official Ireland. The academic Myles Dillon sensed more to their bedside vigil than unconditional love. He noted: 'This policy of compulsory Irish was launched in 1925 and it was inspired, I've long suspected, by the purpose in the minds of the few that pressed for it, of using the language as a means of transferring power – or rather authority. At that time all the cultural institutions of the country, except the National University, were in the hands of the Protestants ... all that must be changed. A new administrative class was to be established and the language was one of the means used.'

As Dillon passed his judgment, the lapel pin called the Fáinne was becoming a must-have accessory amongst the founding class of the Free State to indicate their fluency in the Irish language. There were three grades of Fáinne, meaning ring or circle. The Republican activist Piaras Béaslaí had introduced the scheme in 1911. The first wave of enthusiasm for the Fáinne faded badly, not least because dirt-poor native speakers couldn't afford them. However, a mid-century revival, An Fáinne Nua, proved a resounding success and the pins were a common fashion statement of the wearer's linguistic leanings into the 1970s when they again fell from favour.

The wearing of a Fáinne did not guarantee the admiration of neighbours and colleagues in an Ireland when many had come around to the view of Myles Dillon that it was all much to do with one-upmanship. In 1945, one Francis McConville sent to Taoiseach Éamon de Valera a proposal – now held in the National Archives – for bringing about 'the complete ignorance of English' within decades. In a lengthy and detailed document, he reasoned: 'Only by ensuring that a fresh generation cannot speak English will it be possible to eliminate it as the dominant language.'

While pleading a deep love of his native tongue, he proposed turning the State's schools effectively into internment camps for children. Compulsory purchase orders would be slapped on surrounding buildings to commandeer them for dormitories. McConville insisted that the scheme did not entirely involve breaking up families, because parents would have visiting rights. He wrote: 'The children would still be close to their parents' homes and would readily be seen at suitable times and at regular intervals by the parents. One can readily visualise the results: children at five or six years of age being introduced to such a school and leaving it at, say, fifteen or sixteen or seventeen years of age unable to speak a word of any language but Irish.'

He added: 'Opposition to the restoration of the language should be made a matter of treason against the State.'

The Taoiseach's Departmental Secretary must have suspected the letter was a send-up, but in a climate where it was difficult to tell the crackpot patriot from the sarcastic spoofer he played it straight down the line. Thanking McConville for his proposal, the official wrote back regretting that the leader of the country was 'of the opinion that it would be impossible to get public agreement to a scheme of the magnitude outlined by you'.

54: THE 1916 PROCLAMATION

The Irish Times wasn't above taking money to run an advert for a 'Sinn Féin Revolt Album'.

READERS OF IRISH NEWSPAPERS opened their pages on the bank holiday Monday morning of Easter 1916 to the headline 'Text Of The Proclamation'. The text in question was of a wartime Royal Proclamation issued at London's Windsor Castle warning that any publication or individual leaking a word from secret sessions of the Westminster Parliament would be crushed under the full weight of the law.

The term 'proclamation' was as commonplace in 1916 as 'press statement', 'soundbite' or 'rolling news' today, but in the wake of that Easter weekend the one the whole world was talking about was the Proclamation of the Irish Republic, issued at lunchtime on that fateful Monday. By teatime the capital was plunged into what would become a week of bloodshed and looting.

One week after the Rising began, Dublin's flagship Unionist paper, *The Irish Times*, declared: 'The "Sinn Féin" Insurrection is virtually at an end. Desultory fighting continues in suburban districts. The severity of martial law is maintained; indeed it is increased in the new Proclamation which we print today. Many streets and roads are still dangerous for the careless wayfarer. But the back of the insurrection is broken ... So ends the criminal adventure of the men who declared that they were "striking in full confidence of victory".'

That condemnation appeared on May Day. Five days later the dust had settled and the same newspaper reconstructed the first moments of the rebellion. The piece crowed:

> Few people have heard the beginning of the official declaration of an Irish Republic. Fewer stayed to the end. Though Sackville Street was fairly crowded at the time, the majority of the people paid little attention to the doings of the rebels and preferred the more practical process of looting.
>
> At 1.30 there came from the Post Office a small man in plain clothes with a bundle of papers under his arm. Escorted by a guard of revolutionists he made his way to Nelson's Pillar and began to speak, surrounded by not more than 30 men.

Further on, the report alleged:

> As he gained fervour and thundered out the phrases he had used so often before, his audience became progressively bored. A sweet shop was broken into, and nearly all rushed across the street to join the spoil. A few old men and women who had lost their desire for sweets remained. Even these soon became discontented. 'Isn't Clery's broken into yet?' said one. 'Hivins, it's a great shame Clery's isn't broken.'
>
> On a rumour that this great event was going to happen they moved over to the shop windows and left the speaker finishing his peroration with no one to listen to him but his guard. Like the revolution itself, the proclamation was a great fiasco.

By the time this review appeared on 6 May, eight of the leaders had been executed, with six more to come in the week that followed. The rapidity of the State killings shocked the nation, and the deification of 'criminal adventurers' into heroic martyrs had taken an unstoppable course.

Within another few days a Dubliner called Tom Dolan posted a grim postcard to his sister Dolly in England. The front of the card featured the blasted-out husk of Dublin's Liberty Hall, the rebel stronghold of James Connolly's Citizen Army. On the back of the card was inscribed the cheery scrawl: 'What do you think of this postcard? Just to let you see what Dublin is like. I wish I could get you one of Sackville [Street]. Your loving brother Tom.' Postcards featuring the wreck of the General Post Office had been the first of the set to sell out.

Another few weeks down the line the mood of the country had changed utterly. The rebels of Easter Monday were saints and *The Irish Times* itself wasn't above taking money to run an advert for: 'Sinn Féin Revolt – Album containing over 70 illustrations and full literary record with photographic reproductions of intense interest, price 1/- [one shilling].' Or for the same price, the *Times* reader could have: 'Postcards Sinn Féin Rising – Twelve Views, all different showing destruction caused.'

55 *THE JOY* BY PAUL HOWARD

She spied a pet hedgehog that belonged to one of the porters and whipped the animal into her handbag.

IN THE YEAR 2000 a comic novel appeared entitled *The Miseducation of Ross O'Carroll-Kelly*, which chronicled the misadventures of the engagingly dim schools rugby player of the title. A publishing phenomenon was born which shimmied through the opening decade of the millennium and beyond.

But author Paul Howard's first book in 1996 played out in a place that was the farthest cry imaginable from the leafy, laugh-filled south Dublin stomping ground of the nation's favourite dunderhead.

The Joy was a brutally graphic portrayal of life inside Ireland's most overcrowded and Dickensian prison, Mountjoy Jail in the heart of Dublin's impoverished, heroin-stricken north inner city.

Despite its grim content it flew off the shelves, topping the bestseller listings and earning a place in Irish literary history as the most shoplifted book of all time for reasons that needed no explanation.

When it comes to shoplifting, as with life in general, there is one rule for the rich and one rule for the poor. While those robbing Paul Howard's book to see if they were in it would have good reason to avoid detection, the most notorious kleptomaniac of her day knew that she could pull rank on any victim bold enough to challenge her.

Mary Monckton was the 18th-century wife of the seventh Earl of Cork. Lady Cork was famed for her wit and her lavish dinners, which attracted the likes of Doctor Johnson, Lord Byron and Sir Walter Scott. The guests who attended her soirées were struck by the furniture in her drawing rooms – there was none, apart from dozens of large, handsome armchairs set against the walls which appeared to be nailed down, or glued, or held fast by some other means.

It was when Lady Cork arrived as a guest to the homes of others that her peculiar furnishings began to make some sort of sense. She had an irritating habit of stealing anything that wasn't nailed down.

Lady Cork's 'tendency' became common knowledge in polite society and hosts would hide the good silver and set the table with cheap pewter cutlery. It made no difference – she stole it anyway. Whenever the Lady returned from a visit, part of her maid's duties was to sift through the booty and send it back to its rightful owners.

On one occasion the stolen item was too big to get through the front door: she had arrived home from a party in the horse-drawn carriage of another guest. When the rightful owner turned up the next day she handed it back without an apology, but griping that the steps into it were too high for her short legs.

When she went shopping in London, the tradesmen would never allow their goods to be taken inside her carriage for perusal, as was the custom when dealing with the great and the good. It was always politely but firmly insisted that she go inside the shop and, that done, an assistant would shadow her with an eagle eye while she inspected the wares.

Departing one hotel, she spied a pet hedgehog that belonged to one of the porters. Unable to resist, she whipped the animal into her handbag. After travelling some miles, the hijacked animal began misbehaving, so Lady Cork pulled over at a bakery and swapped it for a sponge cake, having persuaded the baker that hedgehogs make good pest-controllers.

56: A MODEST PROPOSAL

Swift set out reforms that – if the political will were there – would do away with the need for the Irish to sell their offspring for food.

As THE YEAR OF 1729 BEGAN, 61-year-old Jonathan Swift outwardly had every reason to ease himself into a contented retirement. Sitting pretty as the Anglican Dean of St Patrick's Cathedral in Dublin, he was one of Ireland's pre-eminent citizens. During his fifties he had stamped his lasting mark on the world, not once but twice.

Published in 1724–5, his seven pamphlets known as the *Drapier Letters* had forced a world superpower, the British state, into a humiliating climbdown. In 1722 an English ironmonger named William Wood had used his influence at the Royal Court to secure the rights to mint a new coinage for Ireland. By promising handsome kickbacks to members of the King's circle Wood himself stood to make a fortune from his debased coins of inferior materials, which would be ultimately paid for by the Irish merchant and ascendancy classes. Penned anonymously, the *Drapier Letters* launched a furious attack on the scheme, forcing its withdrawal. A State reward was offered for whoever outed Drapier's true identity. The dogs in the street knew it was Swift, but no one was going to grass on Ireland's newest patriotic hero.

Things got even better in 1726 when, with the help of his rich and famous literary friends Alexander Pope, John Arbuthnot and John Gay, Swift arranged the anonymous publication of his greatest masterpiece *Gulliver's Travels*. It became an international sensation, bringing him wealth and, when word got out of the author's identity, great fame and acclaim. Three centuries later *Gulliver's Travels* would become the template for the cultural phenomenon that is *Star Trek*. Gulliver was recast as Captain James T. Kirk boldly going where no man had gone before, while Mr Spock's struggle to reconcile logic and emotion stems from the rift between the Houyhnhnms and the Yahoos.

But wealth and fame did not bring happiness. In 1728 his soulmate Esther Johnson died. She was the 'Stella' of his writings and some scholars believe the two had secretly married.

When 1729 came around Ireland was ravaged by famine after a succession of failed harvests. The streets of Dublin were crowded with ragged skeletal beggars and the colonial administration seemed blithely unable and unwilling to do anything about the sorry state of the nation.

In response, Swift constructed arguably the most macabre, chilling and brilliant satire in the English language. Published anonymously and posing as a straight-faced solution to the plight of Ireland's poor, it was a short pamphlet with a long title, namely: *A Modest Proposal For Preventing The Children Of Poor People In Ireland Being A Burden On Their Parents Or Country, And For Making Them Beneficial To The Publick*.

After setting out the basis of his case, Swift got to the point: 'I have been assured by a very knowing American of my acquaintance in London, that a young healthy child well nursed is at a year old a most delicious nourishing and wholesome food, whether stewed, roast, baked or boiled, and I make no doubt that it will equally serve in a fricassee or a ragout.'

Having argued that the benefits to the poor would include the fact that husbands would cease the practice of beating their pregnant wives for fear of damaging the goods they were carrying, Swift set out a list of reforms that – if the political will were there – would do away with the need for the Irish to sell their offspring for food. These would include taxing absentee landlords who syphoned off the wealth of Ireland but never gave anything back, promoting and supporting the purchase of guaranteed Irish goods instead of squandering money on 'foreign luxury', and 'teaching landlords to have at least one degree of mercy towards their tenants'.

However, having suggested a plan of reforms that would avert the horrors of child slaughter, Swift made plain that he didn't expect to see 'one glimpse of hope' that the ruling classes will take them on board.

Swift's attack on English and Anglo-Irish misrule in Ireland was taken up by many later nationalists as a great patriotic strike for Irish self-determination, but most scholars agree that he was an equal-opportunities hater. His descriptions of the Irish in the Proposal as savage beggars and thieves were echoed in the sermons he gave every week from the pulpit of St Patrick's. Whenever he appeared to address an Irish nation in his writings, he was addressing the Anglo-Irish ascendency to the exclusion of the Catholic masses and the Presbyterian planter stock whom he regarded as dangerous religious and political seditionaries.

In his *Modest Proposal* he refers to peasant newborns being 'dropped' by their mothers, employing a term more apt to livestock. Swift said resentfully that he himself had been 'dropped' in Ireland by his English parents, which he described as a terrible 'misfortune'. The type of pity he seemed most capable of expressing was self-pity.

The impact of Swift's *Modest Proposal* on literature was instant and lasting. Over the following months and years a great vogue grew up for slotting the term 'modest proposal' wherever it could be shoehorned into the titles and texts of new publications. But, for all its searing anger, *A Modest Proposal* was ultimately a loud groan of despair and surrender, of bowing to the inevitable reality that life is not fair.

57: THE IRISH COFFEE

He added a splash of whiskey to the coffees he was serving a shivering party of arrivals from a Pan Am flying boat.

UPON FINISHING HIS FIRST IRISH COFFEE, one self-appointed connoisseur reputedly remarked that the concoction's only drawback was that it ruined three perfectly good drinks – coffee, cream and whiskey. Whatever the merits of that assertion, the drink has become an international symbol of the country to the point where several towns and cities in Ireland and America have been keen to lay claim as its birthplace.

The most vociferous of these is Shannon in County Clare where the beverage has been officially written into the history of Irish aviation. This train of events begins in 1935 when the Free State earmarked a site at Foynes on the mouth of the Shannon for a modern new gateway to Europe in an age when propeller aircraft could only travel so far without refuelling. Next, in 1943, while the world at war delayed the building of Shannon Airport, Joe Sheridan, a chef at the rudimentary Foynes Aerodrome, added a splash of whiskey to the coffees he was serving a shivering party of arrivals disembarking from a Pan Am flying boat which had been forced to turn back to Ireland by bad weather. Then, in 1946 the first scheduled transatlantic flight landed at Shannon Airport. Next, in 1951, Shannon made aviation's next great leap forward when it became the world's first Duty Free airport.

And so on.

A plaque was erected in 1975 to commemorate the invention of Irish coffee at Shannon, and the Airport's present day Sheridan Food Pub also marks the global import of the chef's achievement.

Another Irish coffee achievement which has slipped largely under the radar is that of Irel Coffee, which celebrated 100 years of steady if unspectacular sales in 2013.

Launched into an age when domestic consumers were expected to grind their own beans, Irel was an instant coffee before granules. A thick dark liquid flavoured with chicory, it was to be dripped sparingly into the cup from small bottles with a medicinal look to them. The new product was launched in 1913 by the Johnson Brothers of Dublin. The dark brew was manufactured at their factory in Dublin's Chancery Lane by St Patrick's Cathedral, and the label featured a map of Ireland.

In early 1918 Johnson Brothers sent out cards to Ireland's retailers alerting them to a new marketing push featuring 'a dominating advertisement just now is to be seen on the windows of grocers' shops and also on the trams of Dublin, Belfast, Cork and Londonderry'. The card accompanied two complimentary bottles of the coffee essence. Somewhat optimistically, the message requested: 'If you do not want to put them up on the window please post back to us.'

With its slogan 'Called To The Colours', Irel's manufacturers appeared to nail their own colours firmly to the mast of the United Kingdom's war effort against the Kaiser in the Great War. Three years later, with the War of Independence against membership of that United Kingdom raging in the streets around their factory, Johnson Brothers thought it prudent to take out adverts which stressed their adherence to the nationalist cause.

This time underlining their case with the bold slogan 'Employment', the makers pleaded: 'Irel Coffee is entirely made in Dublin in a factory of scrupulous cleanliness. Every bottle bought gives employment not only in the Irel Factory, but to Irish bottle makers, Irish box makers, Irish printers etc etc.'

More than a century after its launch, Irel Coffee retained a niche place in Irish life as the preferred essence of celebrity chefs and amateur bakers for making a wide range of favourite cakes and desserts.

58: THE PINT BRICK OF ICE CREAM

Its distinctive quality-sealed packaging provided a protection against the rogue ice-cream vendor.

IN THE SUMMER OF 1933 the Dublin dairy owners Hughes Brothers launched their revolutionary pint brick of HB Ice Cream into an Ireland where many people still awaited a first taste of the chilly dessert. The revolutionary bit was to cleverly reverse the normal flow of supply and demand.

To explain …

In the early decades of the 20th century, before the widespread availability of electric refrigeration, ice cream in Ireland was both exclusive and expensive. This was largely to do with the fact that it was made from blocks of ice sawed by hand from the mountain lakes of Norway, and shipped south to London, Dublin and other parts of the then United Kingdom.

By the 1920s factory-made ice was becoming the norm, but ice cream remained a pricy luxury made by a handful of Italian families, mostly confined to Dublin and Cork. Ice cream just didn't travel, so it was generally available only to those within easy reach of one of the Italian parlours in the main cities. Even by the start of the 1930s the only real competition to these family-run parlours were the big Woolworths department stores scattered about the chief population centres, which attracted huge queues for their wimpled cones.

So ice cream had a problem. It couldn't travel to where it was wanted (everywhere), and in the days of horse-and-cart transport the people who wanted it (everyone) couldn't easily get to where it was. HB changed all that in 1933 by taking the ice cream to the people.

The Hughes family's Hazelbrook Farm in rural Rathfarnham was one of Dublin's top milk suppliers in the 1920s, when the three go-ahead Hughes brothers had a bright idea for squeezing added value from their surplus milk and cream. In 1926 they set up Ireland's first ice-cream factory and quickly landed the contract to supply Woolworths and a few smaller outlets.

After a short while, though, it looked like HB might fall victim to its own success. The company could produce far more product than there were shops with the refrigeration to take it. So HB led the way in developing new cold lorries to carry ice cream further afield without melting.

By 1933, the firm had built lines of supply to a network of shops on the outskirts of the capital, recruiting retailers who were connected the mains electricity grid. HB made a simple offer to suitable stores. The company would supply expensive state-of-the-art fridges imported from the United States, on condition that the shopkeeper would only use them to stock HB ice cream. It was a small beginning, but as web of new power lines grew, so would the ice-cream network.

The brick was shrewdly targeted at the new suburbs that were beginning to sprout up around the capital, and by the close of the decade it had become an affordable Sunday treat for many families. As more and more people were uprooted from the crumbling inner city tenements to the new suburbs, having ice cream as a treat after Sunday dinner gained a snob value with the spreading new class of upwardly mobile estate-dwellers. Housewives carried the brick home from the local shop wrapped in newspapers to keep it cool, while shopkeepers carved out individual slices which they sold between wafers (as 'sliders') at twopence a go.

The success of the HB brick wasn't just based on the fact that the after-Mass ice cream had become a status symbol. In its distinctive quality-sealed packaging, it also provided a protection against the rogue ice-cream vendor. At the time the brick was launched, the content of ice cream was barely regulated in Ireland, and what regulations existed were barely enforced. This led to the rise of the dodgy ice-cream dealer who would make up DIY batches – the confectionary equivalent of bathtub gin – and try to sell the stuff before it melted.

Ireland's newspapers reported on one villain found to have caused a poisoning outbreak amongst picnickers: 'The ice cream was being made in a lock-up garage. This had a cement floor and galvanized iron sides and roof, but no other conveniences i.e. no drain, water supply or lighting. The utensils had to be taken home to be washed, and he lived in a back-to-back house which is condemned and waiting to be demolished. It was heavily contaminated with B. coli. Two guinea pigs inoculated from sediment both died within two days.'

59: THE LAMBEG DRUM

The Peep O' Day Boys took their name from the dawn raids they mounted.

THE APPLIANCE OF SONIC SCIENCE has established that the wooden wind instrument of India called the nadaswaram is the planet's loudest acoustic musical apparatus not made of brass, closely followed by various types of bagpipes and the jumbo-sized Lambeg Drum, which takes its name from the County Antrim village of the same name. Such is the weight and unwieldy size and shape of the drum that scaled-down versions have become increasingly popular over recent decades with the Orange marchers who commemorate key historical events in a season of raucous street celebrations that runs from the beginning of July (the 1916 Battle of the Somme) to the week before Christmas (the 1688 Siege of Derry).

The Orange Order emerged in 1795 from a group of community activists called the Orange Boys who were, in turn, an offshoot of the older Peep O' Day Boys which formed around 1779 as tensions mounted between Protestants and Catholics over control of the lucrative linen trade. The Peep O' Day Boys took their name from the dawn raids they launched to smash looms and destroy linen webs in an effort to eliminate creeping Catholic competition. Having prevailed against a mob calling themselves The Catholic Defenders in the pre-arranged Battle of The Diamond in Armagh in 1795 – reportedly killing 30 Defenders while sustaining no losses in return – the Orange Boys reconstituted themselves as the Orange Order.

In the year following the foundation of the Orange Order, thousands of Catholics were driven out of County Armagh by elements associated with the Peep O' Day Boys. The Orange Order distanced itself from the Protestant offensive and claimed that no Peep O' Day Boy was ever admitted to the association, although in his 2007 history of the Order the BBC journalist Mervyn Jess conceded that some 'may have slipped through the net'.

60: GAELTACHT ROAD SIGNS (BLACKED OUT)

English-language saboteurs now took to sneaking around under cover of darkness.

IN 2002 FIANNA FÁIL'S Éamon Ó Cuív took over as Minister for Community, Rural and Gaeltacht Affairs from his first cousin Síle de Valera. He entered the office at a time when Irish-language activists were waging a guerrilla war on bilingual road signs in several designated Irish-speaking districts. In 2004, for instance, in a fresh wave of signage sabotage, it was reported that the English version of place names and directions had been blotted out with black paint in the Cork townland of Ballyvourney and its surrounding Gaeltacht hinterland.

The following year the Minister decreed that signposts in Gaeltacht areas would from now on feature place names in Irish only. The residents of Dingle in County Kerry learned that under the new dispensation their town would henceforth be known by the sole name of An Daingean. This diktat met with a mixed response. Those opposed to the change pointed out that the name Dingle had brand recognition around the world and that the switch could do untold damage to the tourist trade there. Besides, they told the Minister, there was already a Daingean in County Offaly.

After much heated debate, a compromise was reached. The town would now be known as Dingle/Daingean Uí Chúis, but the Irish-only signs directing vital tourist traffic would remain unaltered. This unsatisfactory solution led to a reverse of the earlier trend, as English-language saboteurs now took to sneaking around under cover of darkness spraying 'Dingle' on the road signs.

One prominent Galway figure of the previous generation had come out against putting up road signs in rural Ireland as a matter of general principle.

The driving test was introduced in 1964. The following year Fine Gael's John Donnellan supported a 30mph speed limit for the city of Dublin, but said that restricting cars to 30mph on rural roads would be 'a great waste of time' for drivers in a hurry. He objected to the waste of public money on 'too many signs' and argued: 'One of these 30mph signs is quite sufficient for any town.'

He raised his objections in the Dáil, telling his fellow deputies:

> I want to refer to the 30mph speed limit signs. In the first place, I do not think these signs should be so far away from the main towns. In some cases they are almost two miles outside the towns and in other cases a mile. In the case of some towns, they are quite near. I fully agree with the idea of having a 30mph speed limit in Dublin but, for the ghost towns between here and the west of Ireland, it is a great

waste of time to have a 30mph speed limit – you could have a 40 miles per hour speed limit for them.

Furthermore, there are too many signs in the country. I do not know whether these signs were erected by private contract or by the county councils in co-operation with the Department of Local Government but if it was done by private contract then it was a damn good job and a great source of revenue to some individual or some bunch of individuals. One of these 30mph signs is quite sufficient for any town.

But his pleas were ignored and the powerful road-sign lobby had their way.

61: THE JACK CHARLTON MUG

The accusation that the blow-ins couldn't tell one end of a ball from the other did not deter them.

WHEN THE FIRST SQUAD to represent an independent Ireland in a major tournament set off for the finals of football's World Championships in Paris in 1924 there was no big send-off. While a smattering of friends and family waved off the team as they sailed away on their great adventure, the Free

State government cold-shouldered the nation's latest ambassadors with something approaching contempt.

The young Football Association of Ireland (FAI) was strapped for cash, and since the Paris tournament was an Olympic event the body had expected some funding from the Irish Olympic Committee (IOC). However, the chief of the IOC, J. J. Keane, was a dyed-in-the-wool GAA man who strongly believed that for Ireland to allow itself be represented in a soccer tournament was to bring shame and dishonour on the newly liberated Gaelic nation.

The FAI managed to scrape together the funding, not just to send 16 players and a trainer to Paris, but also to pay for six officials to shuffle the paperclips. One of the players, Ernie Crawford, was also captain of the Irish rugby team. When Crawford's kitbag was searched by French customs, officials found a pistol concealed in his gear. He explained that he carried it for protection.

Despite the repeated failure of the national team to qualify for a major final, or show any level of consistency, and despite the hostility of the school system and Official Ireland in general, soccer retained a loyal grass-roots following. In 1955, 22,000 people converged on Dublin's Dalymount Park to watch Ireland play communist Yugoslavia in defiance of a declaration by Archbishop John Charles McQuaid that Catholics should boycott the fixture.

During the 1960s big games in the League of Ireland could attract attendances of 20,000 to 30,000. By the early 1970s English TV coverage began to deplete severely the numbers at domestic matches, but this trend was reversed for a brief time when big stars nearing the end of their careers, including George Best, Bobby Tambling, Gordon Banks and Bobby Charlton, energised the League of Ireland on a pay-per-play basis.

Throughout these bleak years, however, the national team remained the Nearly Men of European football, and in bad times the Not Even Nearly Men. A laboured qualifying campaign for the 1986 World Cup in Mexico ended with a 4-1 home thrashing by the Danes. As the closing credits rolled on the coverage, the RTÉ continuity announcer remarked sourly: 'And there'll be more comedy after the break in *Cheers*.'

There was more comedy shortly afterwards when the FAI set about the business of replacing departed manager Eoin Hand. At the end of the selection fiasco, England World Cup winner Jack Charlton was the last man standing, although by that point he'd half forgotten he was a candidate at all. Charlton and his back-room team used the 'grandmother rule' to recruit a fresh draft of British-born players with instant success. When the Republic qualified for the Euro '88 Finals in West Germany a vibrant new cottage industry in mugs, scarves, caps, T-shirts and anything else that would take an imprint of the cheesy Charlton grin got up and running.

But the glee that accompanied Euro '88 was just the warm-up for the mass hysteria that followed when the team qualified for the Italia '90 World Cup Finals.

In the summer of 1990 Italy capitulated before an invasion by a mass movement called Jack's Army whose very existence was resented and ridiculed by the 'real' supporters who'd paid their dues freezing on dank terraces stoically swallowing cruel doses of grinding disappointment. The accusation that the blow-ins couldn't tell one end of a ball from the other didn't deter the tens of thousands who sold their grannies to go to Italy for the three group games, and then stayed put as the magical mystery tour kept going.

The 'real' supporters were not the only ones to cast jaundiced eyes upon the carnival. One English newspaper branded the Irish set-up as 'Jack Charlton's team of international misfits'. No one cared, perhaps because there was a morsel of substance to the charge. When Taoiseach Charles Haughey arrived into the dressing room after the narrow defeat to Italy in Rome which ended the great adventure, one English-born player asked another, 'Who's he?' The reply came: 'I don't know, but I think he owns a tea-shop.'

For many years after Jack Charlton received his marching orders, cheap mugs bearing his grinning mug continued to share shelf space with the finest china in homes all across the land.

62: THE BALLOT PAPER

She said that if she couldn't vote for the Archbishop she would vote for no one.

WHEN THE IRISH FREE STATE joined the ranks of the world's electoral democracies in the early 1920s it was joining a relatively exclusive club. During that decade between the wars democracy was not the norm, nor even the ideal, that it was to become after the Second World War.

Out of 64 independent states on the planet in the early 1920s, only 21, including Ireland, were functioning democracies. Some, like Italy and Germany, would abandon the experiment of tolerating the ballot box within a decade. Democracy was fragile and in a largely peasant society like Ireland many held strong reservations about the potential the democratic process contained for shackling the natural order of tribal loyalties.

The 1923 general election took place shortly after the end of the Civil War, and that deep gash in Irish society was still weeping. On the day the people went to vote a scuffle broke out at a south Dublin polling booth where grocer's assistant Thomas Tynan was arrested on a charge that he had 'accosted voters, taking from them their cards and marking them as to how each individual was to vote, thereby obstructing the voters at the polling booth'. Tynan was hauled before a judge where his lawyer argued that since his client had not attempted to impersonate any of those he had interfered with (the crime of personation), he hadn't broken any law. The judge agreed and threw out the case.

In the Wicklow village of Glendalough in the same election, voting proceeded without incident until around noon, when a group of armed men descended on the polling station and insisted on helping out the Free State soldiers on guard duty there. The uninvited freelance militia refused to disperse until the Army sent in reinforcements to relieve them.

In some cases, voters just didn't 'get' the whole voting thing. In Kilkenny, an elderly woman insisted on casting her vote for Dr Daniel Mannix. Polling clerks politely explained to her that Dr Mannix was not a candidate in her constituency nor in any other, since his time was fully taken up by his job as the Catholic Archbishop of Melbourne in faraway Australia. On hearing this, the woman said that if she couldn't vote for Archbishop Mannix she would vote for no one, before leaving in an indignant huff.

Early Free State electioneering was not for the faint hearted. After the 1927 campaign, a Fianna Fáil TD charged that, on the say-so of the Cumann na nGaedheal government, the police in Kerry had torn down his party's posters, commandeered Fianna Fáil election cars, roughed up election workers and confiscated electoral registers from Fianna Fáil personation officers keeping an eye out for rivals' attempts to cheat.

After the 1932 general election it was Fianna Fáil's turn in power, and soon the party was itself the target of routine denunciations that it was soft on personation. From the opposition benches the ousted government fired off Dáil questions demanding to know why prosecutions for electoral fraud plummeted after it lost office. One deputy asked the Justice Minister, rhetorically: 'Is it due to the fact that his party is kept in office by reason of this abominable practice?'

Fine Gael routinely attacked Fianna Fáil for interfering with the judicial process, with the Minister for Justice exercising his lawful 'prerogative of mercy' to have court sentences for personation reduced or quashed. The government response was sometimes one of open contempt. In 1934 Fine Gael tabled a question asking how many times the Minister had exercised the prerogative in the preceding period. Five times, said the Minister. The FG deputy asked disbelievingly: 'Was that all?' 'Oh no,' smirked the Minister. 'There were some before that.'

By 1960 electoral fraud had become a hard currency of Irish

politics, and when Fianna Fáil's opponents levelled the routine charge that the party encouraged its loyalists to 'vote early and vote often', the comments were never entirely in jest. Independent Deputy Frank Sherwin complained to the Justice Minister that year: 'There are at least 25,000 voters personated at every election and the Gardaí do not act. How many persons were imprisoned for personation in the last general election? None. Personation is treated as a joke.'

The Minister joked dismissively: 'Judging by what the Deputy says, some members of this House must have got in that way!'

Which was precisely the point that Sherwin was making. He thundered on: 'All the parties treat it as a joke, that is why the Act is broken in 1,001 ways and no one is ever charged. The parties behave like gangsters in Chicago. They look upon it as their business.'

The biggest personation sensation of them all hit the headlines on 18 February 1982 when the election agent of Fianna Fáil leader Charles Haughey, Pat O'Connor, was charged with attempting to vote at two polling stations in the tight Dublin North constituency. By lunchtime on polling day the damaging news was splashed across the front of the early edition of the *Evening Herald*. Mysterious buyers mobilised with lightning speed, snapping up every copy in bulk from newsagents in the constituency.

Just as the six o'clock TV news went on air, and with many people returning home from work and still to go to the polls, the district suffered a widespread power blackout. Locals said that someone had thrown a bicycle into an ESB transformer. A judge later cleared Haughey's henchman (now jokingly known as Pat O'Connor Pat O'Connor), on the grounds that a secret ballot makes it impossible to tell if someone has voted once, never mind twice.

63 THE SAFE CROSS CODE BOOKLET

If Mister Careless Goes To Town had been made 50 years later it would have been retitled Mister Careless Goes to Jail.

IN 1970 THE BRITISH GOVERNMENT launched a multimedia road safety campaign under the title the Green Cross Code, which came with a catchy instructional ditty of the same name. In an effort to attract the maximum attention of Britain's schoolchildren it recruited the talents of the likeable *Jackanory* storyteller Bernard Cribbins, the much-loved animated squirrel Tufty Fluffytail, and the muscle-bound future Darth Vader David Prowse as the Green Cross Man.

RTÉ soon followed suit with a suspiciously similar road safety campaign called The Safe Cross Code. Instead of a bushy squirrel the home station had a fluffy mutt familiar to children everywhere as Judge from *Wanderly Wagon*. Instead of a man mountain in a superhero's outfit, RTÉ signed up stage schoolboy Brendan Grace to sing the song that began: 'Look for a safe place ...' The scheme was a big hit with the nation's primary pupils because, in addition to the colourful brochure containing the lyrics, they got a metal badge featuring their favourite dog, plus a welcome break in lessons when some smiling ambassador from the outside world came in to run the promotional footage on the school's reel-to-reel projector.

Two of the most intriguing public information films of the mid-20th century were produced by the Catholic Church to address two very disparate issues close to the hearts of the priesthood. One, from the 1960s, entitled *Good Manners In Church*, sought to curb bad practices such as loitering down the back during Mass, stepping out for a sly smoke, and sneaking off home during Communion. Another from the 1970s borrowed a trendy title from a Rory Gallagher album entitled *Messing With The Kids*. The title would take on unfortunate undertones in later times, but the intent behind the film was to reassure concerned parents that just because their youngsters liked rock music it didn't necessarily make them Satan worshippers.

Most public information films from the 1940s to the 1980s sought to reform our drinking, our driving, or our tendency to attempt both at the same time. The 1970s short entitled *Smash The Round System* climaxed with a dramatic fist coming down like a judge's gavel on a table of pints. *Just The Two Will Do* from the 1980s advised motorists that two pints or shorts was their safe limit.

The 1949 film *Mister Careless Goes To Town* begins with the title character ploughing into the back of a stalled vehicle because he's not paying attention while driving too fast. Next we find him blithely parking in a space clearly marked No Waiting until a guard moves him on. He then drives erratically through the streets of Dublin until he is stopped by a traffic policeman at Butt Bridge for attempting to make a wrong turn. Undeterred, he parks illegally at a bus stop and goes off to a pub for a few scoops. On his merry way home he crashes his car and ends up having to make a court appearance.

If *Mister Careless Goes To Town* had been made 50 years later it would have been retitled *Mister Careless Goes to Jail*.

64: DUBLIN'S SPIRE

The natives dubbed the would-be bathing beauty 'The Floozie in the Jacuzzi'.

FOR OVER 150 YEARS Dubliners were embroiled in a love-hate relationship with Nelson's Pillar which dominated the capital's main artery from the time it went up in 1809. Erected to commemorate Admiral Nelson's victory against the French at the Battle of the Nile in 1798, it became known as the 'city sofa' because idle citizens would lounge on its steps watching the world go by.

However, as the tide of nationalist sentiment rose towards the close of the Victorian era, Lord Nelson in his crow's nest came more and more to resemble a Big Brother reminder of what patriots had now started calling 'the slave mind'. In 1891 Dublin's Lord Mayor introduced a Bill at the Westminster Parliament for the removal of what W. B. Yeats described as 'a monstrosity'. The proposal was scotched by Dublin Corporation on grounds of expense.

Nelson's Pillar survived the 1916 Rising, the War of Independence and the Civil War with barely a scratch, but at the start of March 1966 it crashed to earth with a bang. The 50th anniversary of the Easter Rising was just weeks away and the demolition of Nelson was greeted as a warm-up for the main event by that large part of the populace already whipped up into a patriotic fervour by the country's leadership.

As Dubliners danced in the rubble, many of them making away with bits and pieces for souvenirs, a Garda spokesman gave the bomb attack the thumbs-up as 'a thorough job'. Not quite. An ugly stump jutted up from the country's main street. A few days later the

Irish Army destroyed the remainder of the Pillar with a controlled explosion that, disappointingly, was not as controlled as it might have been. The terrorist explosion had caused no collateral damage and, miraculously, no injuries. The lawful blast shattered just about every shop front in the vicinity, obliging the forces of law and order to try to prevent an orgy of looting by the large crowd of spectators who'd gathered.

In the weeks and months that followed the toppling of the Pillar, the government and the newspaper letters pages were snowed under with suggestions for Nelson's replacement. These included statues of Michael Collins, Pádraig Pearse, Saint Patrick, a winged figure, an eternal flame 'to commemorate all those who died for Ireland' and an underground chapel dedicated to the blood sacrifice of the rebels of Easter 1916.

The announcement in the autumn of 1979 that Pope John Paul II was to visit Ireland sparked a revival of the campaign to replace Nelson with a monument in the centre of the capital that would proclaim Ireland's Christianity. Members of the faithful began a daily vigil on the traffic island where the Pillar had once stood, praying aloud for the authorities to build a 'triumphalist' structure on the site that would feature some combination of 'Christ, the Blessed Virgin Mary, Joseph the Worker and the Dove' (the Holy Spirit).

In the event, the civic authorities let the opportunity pass. The prime space remained vacant until 1988 when Dublin's civic authorities held a series of street parties to commemorate its 1,000th birthday, in the face of stern objections from the massed ranks of historians who insisted that AD 988 had been plucked from the air as a convenient peg for getting in the tourist spend.

So, to mark the city's pretend millennium, Dublin Corporation green-lighted a sculpture commissioned by businessman Michael Smurfitt in memory of his father. Intended as the personification of the River Liffey, and named for a figure in James Joyce's *Finnegans Wake*, the Anna Livia Plurabelle sculpture featured a young woman lolling, clothed in a sloping, flowing bath.

From the outset, Nelson's belated replacement met with derision from the natives who labelled it 'a carbuncle' and dubbed the would-be bathing beauty 'The Floozie in the Jacuzzi'. The Floozie was removed in 2001 to make way in 2003 for The Monument of

Light, better known as The Spire, The Spike or The Stiletto In The Ghetto. When the shiny silver-foil column was finally erected, local wits, referring to Ireland's most famous department store across the street, suggested its theme song should be 'I Can See Clery's Now The Crane Has Gone'.

65: THE MGM LION

Dublin-born Slats was the roaring mascot that opened and closed every MGM presentation.

DUBLIN ZOO OPENED ITS GATES in 1831 with a modest menagerie of just 46 animals and 72 birds and a stiff entry fee of sixpence which served to keep out the riff-raff. Only when the admission price was dropped to one penny for Sundays did the attraction become truly woven into the social fabric of the city.

Many of the founders of the Royal Zoological Society of Dublin were practising medics with an ulterior motive. Before the passing of the Anatomy Act of 1832 it was illegal to dissect a human body unless it had formerly been inhabited by an executed criminal – a law which ensured a brisk trade in grave robbing – so in the first year of Dublin Zoo's existence there was a waiting list amongst its patrons to take a scalpel to the primates as they reached their natural end.

While Dublin Zoo owned its own lions, tigers and pumas during its early years, it had to rent some of its marquee beasts from travelling circuses. An elephant was secured on loan from London Zoo in 1836. Once the Zoo's livestock levels reached critical mass it established a reputation as one of the world's great breeding centres for exotic wildlife. In the two decades from 1857 to 1876 Dublin produced 92 lion cubs at a time when the wholesale slaughter of the species was gathering steam in Africa.

Queen Victoria became the Zoo's patron in the year of her coronation, 1837, and she would pay a visit in 1900. Before that, the gardens' most distinguished visitor was former United States President Ulysses S. Grant who took a particular interest in the lions. Grant had mentored the rise and rise of Philip Sheridan to the role of Commander of the US Army. Sheridan, whose parents emigrated from Leitrim, is infamous for saying: 'The only good injun's a dead injun.' (Or, depending on your source: 'The only good Indians I ever saw were dead.' Or, if Sheridan himself was to be believed, he never said it at all.)

Dublin Zoo relied on its glamorous lion-breeding programme to generate funds for its more mundane day-to-day expenses. Its most famous export in this regard, according to ill-founded Hollywood lore, was Slats, born in 1919 and sold to the Goldwyn Pictures Corporation in Hollywood where these fierce creatures were always in demand for jungle adventures. Slats was supposedly trained by Hollywood's premier animal trainer Volney Phifer just in time for the merging of Goldwyn with two other studios to become Metro-Goldwyn-Mayer. Slats and his trainer toured the United States to promote the launch of MGM. The story goes that between 1924 and 1928 Dublin-born Slats was the roaring mascot that opened and closed every MGM presentation – except in those silent movie days the roar had to be imagined.

Hollywood lore has it that Slats and his trainer struck up an uncommonly close bond and that when the lion died in 1936 Phifer buried his favourite on his farm. Phifer marked Slats' grave with a granite slab and a pine tree in order to, in the trainer's words, 'hold down the lion's spirit'. Slats' successor, Jackie, who would become the famed roaring lion of MGM's golden age, got his job because he was a dead ringer for the lion from Dublin Zoo.

As the kings of the jungle and the top of the food chain, the lions at Dublin Zoo tended to get preferential treatment when hard decisions had to be made. When the Easter Rising broke out in 1916 the Zoo was poorly stocked to withstand a week without fresh food supplies, so some dingoes, some goats and an elderly donkey were amongst the display items that had to be sacrificed for the greater good.

The dark days of 'The Emergency' (the Second World War to the rest of the planet) brought further desperate measures. In 1943, appealing for help from the public, one of the wardens revealed that a python had just been fed a meal that must last it for five weeks. He confessed: 'It was a dead swan from the Sloblands, oil covered when brought in, but clipped and animated for the reptile's benefit.'

The war ended, but for an Ireland on its economic knees the shortages did not. In 1954 Dublin Zoo invited compassionate individuals or firms to adopt 'lonely animals' by sponsoring their feed and upkeep for a year. An elephant would cost around £200; a lion, tiger or sea lion £100; a leopard or puma £50 and so on. In return, the sponsor could have their name on the animal's cage.

The Zoo was forced to make the appeal because, with the economy flatlining, attendance revenue was down and the cost of feeding the animals had soared. An official revealed that one holiday company with a beaver on its logo had made inquiries about adopting one of the water-going rodents. However, he remarked: 'At the moment we have no beaver but we hope to get one.' The official expressed concern that with horsemeat so scarce and pricy, the Zoo might soon have to start feeding the lions on whale meat.

66: THE MARIAN GROTTO

One shop extended its opening hours to cater for the invasion of the statue watchers.

IN SEPTEMBER 1953 Pope Pius XII declared that 1954 would be the very first Marian Year in the long history of the Catholic Church. The faithful were asked to engage in twelve months of commemorations dedicated to the Virgin Mary. The Pope urged Catholics to make a pilgrimage to Marian churches and Marian shrines, 'or at least an altar in which the sacred image of the Blessed Virgin Mary is enshrined'.

The Papal appeal sparked a small building boom across Ireland as members of the faithful mobilised to erect shrines, statues and replicas of the Lourdes Grotto in parishes from Malin Head in the north to Mizen Point in the south.

One of those who rose to the challenge of building a place of worship was the 50-year-old proprietor of Nash's Pub in the tiny Cork hamlet of Ballinspittle. He selected a spot on a steep hillside along the busy-ish Ballinspittle-to-Cork road, and the grotto was completed in 1956.

Nothing much happened at the Ballinspittle shrine for the next 29 years, until July 1985 when, as darkness began fell, two parishioners thought they saw the statue of Mary move as they said the Rosary. Clare O'Mahony reported: 'It was as if the statue was breathing and the hands moved.' Within days hundreds of people were gathering throughout the night, with more and more claiming to see the Virgin 'moving to and fro'.

Inside the first week, the transport company CIÉ was laying on special services, temporary toilets were being erected and Telecom Éireann was making plans to erect three new phone boxes in the village. Inside the first week, too, rival claims of moving statues were reported from the nearby villages of Dunmanway and Courtmacsherry, but these were dismissed by the many faithful who continued to make a beeline for Ballinspittle.

Eight days after the first reported movements, crowds of 5,000 were showing up daily, travelling from all parts of Ireland and abroad. At this point, with hundreds of witnesses claiming to have seen the statue swaying from the shoulders up, the local Bishop delivered his Church's first official response. Warning that 'direct supernatural intervention is a very rare happening in life', Bishop Michael Murphy insisted that 'all natural explanations would have to be examined and exhausted over a lengthy period'.

Newspaper reports noted that Ballinspittle's two pubs and its shops were doing a roaring tourist trade, and that one of the shops had extended its opening hours to cater for the invasion of the statue watchers, with the incoming traffic now backed up as far as the eye could see. Not every visitor was welcome. As *The Irish Times* reported: 'Attempts by one enterprising chip van owner to cater for the crowds were quickly halted by the locals who regard the intruder's activities as unsuitable to the solemnity of the occasion.'

Banned from the commercial heart of the action, the fast-food vans made camp on the perimeter close to a number of car parks which had sprung up overnight. One cheeky cardboard sign advertised 'a Madonna Burger'. A man wearing a peaked cap and directing vehicles with a torch into a mucky field signposted Car Park, told a reporter that his work was 'all voluntary, every bit of it'. Asked why, if his efforts were all voluntary, he was charging £1 per car per night, he explained it was to cover the cost of opening the field for parking.

One national newspaper cynically connected Ballinspittle's moving statue with 'the poor tourist season', further observing: 'The movement occurred mostly after 10pm. Was there drink involved?'

Five academics from the Department of Applied Psychology at University College Cork quickly intervened to say that on foot of experiments they'd carried out, they had ascertained that the movement was all a trick of the light. The academics argued that a person sways when standing still for even a short time, so that whatever they're looking at appears to move. In daylight conditions a person can check whether it is themselves or the object they are looking at which is moving by fixing it against another static object. The Ballinspittle Virgin only moved when the darkness made it impossible for the viewers to fix it against the background. Getting a fix was made doubly difficult by the lights trained on the statue and the glow from the lit-up halo, producing a glare that blurred the surroundings.

Rejecting these findings, one resident of Ballinspittle dismissed the scientists as 'maniacs'. Across the Atlantic, *The Wall Street Journal* quoted the Irish government press secretary as saying: 'Three quarters of the country is laughing heartily.' Five weeks after the first sighting, RTÉ received 'a steady flow' of letters from viewers claiming to have seen an apparition of Christ appear on their TV screens during a *Nine O'Clock News* report on Ballinspittle.

In mid-September the National Road Safety Association issued a very belated warning that 'dangerously parked' vehicles at rural shrines would 'almost certainly' lead to a jump in accidents.

In fact, by the time the Road Safety body got into gear the approaching winter was bringing a natural close to the season of statue watching, and there was never to be a summer quite like it again.

67: KERRYGOLD BUTTER

One of Cromwell's chief enforcers asserted that the Irish were very fond of 'butter made rancid by keeping in bogs'.

A GENTLY RISING TIDE in the economy at the start of the 1960s encouraged the Irish Dairy Board to try something new. For decades, the vast majority of the country's foodstuffs had been exported in the raw, usually to Britain, for value-added processing, packaging and branding. Kerrygold Butter would be something else. Manufactured and packaged in Ireland, it would be a rare experiment in direct marketing to the wider world. The name was chosen to conjure up images of natural goodness and sun-kissed pastures, with romantic Ireland itself pitched as the unique selling point.

The butter was belatedly launched on the domestic market in 1972 with a lavish advertising campaign under the triumphal heading 'Welcome Home Kerrygold!' By then the brand had built up a head of steam abroad over the course of a decade of relentless marketing. But the Dairy Board had not been at all sure of their product at the beginning, confining its initial launch to the tiny district of Winter Hill in the north of England in 1962.

The doubts surrounding the substance known as Bog Butter have been around for much longer. Bog Butter, as the name suggests, is butter that is occasionally dug up in bogs. Of some 450 known lodes found in Europe, the vast majority have turned up in Ireland and Scotland, with a scattering of examples stretching from the Faroe Islands across Scandinavia to Kashmir and Assam in modern-day India. Some scientists refer to the societies that engage in the burial practice as 'butter eaters'.

One of the earliest people to essay a scientific study of Irish bog butter was Sir William Wilde, father of Oscar, who noted that one of Cromwell's chief enforcers in Ireland, William Petty, had asserted that the natives were very fond of 'butter made rancid by keeping in bogs'. Wilde additionally quoted from James Farewell's uncomplimentary poem 'The Irish Hudibras', which stated: 'Butter to eat with their hog / Was seven years buried in a bog.'

In an 1856 address to the Irish Natural Society, Wilde reported: 'When I originally read the statement of Petty I came to the conclusion that he was wrong, and that this bog butter was much older than his time, but I have learned to correct that opinion. Why or wherefore the people put their butter in bogs I cannot tell, but it is a fact that great quantities of this substance have been found in the bogs, and that it has invariably assumed the physical and chemical characters presented by the specimen now before the Academy. It is converted into a hard, yellowish-white substance, like old Stilton cheese, and in taste resembling spermaceti [wax found in the head of sperm whales]. It is, in fact, changed into the animal substance denominated "adipocere".'

Adipocere, also known as 'grave wax', consists of animal fat. Recent scientific tests suggest that the dairy butter did not, in fact, change into this fleshy substance, but that both butter and meat from animals were buried separately in bogland.

Scientists still argue over the precise mechanisms by which bogs preserve animal and vegetable matter, but it is agreed that the lack of oxygen retards the breakdown of material. Because the Irish traditionally made their butter without the salt which was common elsewhere, the bog may have served the same preservative function. In their 1805 book *Travels In Iceland*, Classen and Povelson reported that the Icelandic peasantry stored away butter during the milking season and dug it up in the winter as 'sour butter'. Although it could become acidic over time, this sour butter was edible after 20 years in the ground.

Iceland was discovered by Irish monks who had sailed north-west from their settlement on the Faroe Islands, and a noted early historian of the Faroes, L. J. Debes, wrote in 1670 that the islanders gathered goat's cheese for preservation and then 'cut it in pieces, and allowed to rot awhile. It was then rendered, and cast into large pieces, which they dig and put in moist earth to keep it, it growing the better the longer it is kept, and when it is old and is cut, it tasteth like old cheese.'

This suggests that at least some bog butter was laid down like a vintage wine or cheese to age it as a delicacy for the tables of the well-to-do. And if it was a valued delicacy, that was another good reason for keeping it hidden in the earth. In Sweden, butter was collected as a form of tax, while a 15th-century manuscript from Scotland reported that 16 horse-loads of butter and cheese were found buried close to the house of a tenant engaged in the business of tax avoidance.

68: THE ELECTION POSTER

The posters called for private facilities for alcoholic TDs, suppression of the Irish language and easy divorce.

IN JUNE 1922 THE COUNTRY went to the polls in a general election that would be a referendum on a Treaty drawn up by Britain that offered independence to 26 counties of Ireland on condition that six of the Ulster counties would remain part of the United Kingdom.

Going into the election Sinn Féin found itself in the unique position of being both the party of government in Dáil Éireann, and the party of opposition. The President of the party, Éamon de Valera, vehemently opposed ratifying the Treaty signed by Michael Collins, which fell short of delivering a 32-county Irish Republic. Collins maintained that the Treaty offered 'the freedom to achieve freedom', and a majority in his party took the same pragmatic view. De Valera was defeated when the pro-Treaty members of the Dáil approved the deal with Britain by the slim margin of 64 to 57.

The British insisted that before they would withdraw from the 26 counties, the Provisional Government must secure popular approval for the Treaty. Fearing outright Civil War, the two feuding sides of Sinn Féin hatched a gentleman's agreement that the Treaty would not be overtly an issue in the poll, although in reality it would be the only issue.

Just before polling day, the Provisional Government of Arthur Griffith and Michael Collins broke the gentleman's agreement and plastered the land with arguably the most striking and potent poster in the history of Irish elections. It kicked off: 'You can get the Republic for all Ireland through the safe and sure method of the Treaty or you can try another round through the alphabet of miseries.

A – Auxiliaries.
B – Black and Tans.
C – Commandeering.
D – Deaths.
E – Executions.
F – Fatalities.
G – Gallows.
H – Hangings.
I – Internments.
J – Jails.
K – Knoutings (Whippings).
L – Licence (Disregard of the law).
M – Murders.
N – Nerve Strain.
O – Oppression.
P – Persecution.

Q – Questioning.
R – Raids.
S – Spies.
T – Threats.
U – Usurpation.
V – Vandalism.
W – Wails.
X, Y, Z – The final horrors which words cannot describe.'

The Irish public got the message and approved the Treaty deal by a landslide.

Eleven years on in 1933, having recently lost office after commendably getting the new Free State standing on its own feet, the successors to Griffith and Collins in Cumann na nGaedheal showed they were once again one step ahead of their rivals in media savvy when the Fianna Fáil government called a snap election.

One newspaper reported: 'An interesting electioneering device that has been prepared by Cumann na nGaedheal for the remoter areas is a talking film, which includes a speech by Mister Cosgrave lasting about fifteen minutes. This will be submitted to the Film Censor for his approval and it will be sent immediately on tour to smaller places which Mister Cosgrave will be unable to reach.' The party political short was road-tested at an open-air event in the Dublin fishing village of Howth and was a great success. 'People around the meeting place were able to remain at the windows of their homes and see and hear the speakers without any difficulty.'

Sadly for Cumann na nGaedheal, the public's thumbs-up for the movie didn't translate to the ballot box.

Almost half a century later in 1977, the feel-good factor was at last sweeping the land as Fianna Fáil spun the greatest giveaway story ever told, with a manifesto promising the abolition of household rates and the end of motor tax, with the sun, moon and stars to come a little later. The giddy mood even infected the business of postering, when, on the eve of polling day, startling placards went up in Dublin seeking votes for Labour's Conor Cruise O'Brien.

The posters put forward a surprise package of measures even more surprising than the Fianna Fáil promises which Conor Cruise O'Brien himself had denounced as 'blatant electoral fraud'. The

O'Brien placards called for: 'Abortion on demand. Private facilities for alcoholic TDs. Suppression of the Irish language. Easy divorce. Legalisation of drugs. Congolese call girls.'

The outgoing Minister was outraged that his name had been taken in vain. He fumed: 'This is clearly a black propaganda campaign aimed at damaging the Labour Party. The fact that the printed posters have been widely and quickly distributed shows that there is an organisation behind this scurrilous and despicable campaign. We call on the Fianna Fáil party, on the eve of this election, to repudiate and condemn this vile propaganda.' No one in Fianna Fáil stepped forward to take the blame, or the credit.

69: FRY'S CHOCOLATE CREAM

'The actors thought I hated them. Too bloody true.'

I N THE YEARS BEFORE TELEVISION started up in Ireland in 1961, the sponsored radio shows on Raidió Éireann occupied a place in the national conversation that has no counterpart in today's fragmented multimedia world.

It's doubtful that there was a single water cooler in the country at the time. If there had been, the hot gossip twice a week would have been the latest developments in the nation's favourite soap, *The Kennedys of Castleross*, set in a drab midlands town based on

Mullingar. Instead, that gossip was exchanged in the queue at the grocer's counter, at the parish pump, or on the stroll home from morning Mass. Sponsored by Fry-Cadbury the radio drama first aired in 1955 and quickly took a vice-like grip on the public's imagination. Every Tuesday and Thursday at one o'clock, stores, factories and farms stopped for tea as the entire nation eavesdropped on the latest gossip from Mrs Kennedy's corner shop.

The very first dramatic dilemma in the very first episode of *The Kennedys* hinged on the fact that Mrs Kennedy couldn't oblige a valued customer, Mrs Shaw, who was on the phone wishing to have a bag of sweets delivered. The young Hugh Leonard, later a distinguished dramatist, came on board early on to write scripts for the princely sum of eight guineas per episode, which was almost as much as he was taking home each week from his day job in the civil service.

The writers were tightly constricted by unbreakable ground rules, such as the one dictating that Mrs Kennedy must always be at the centre of the action. After her, for no apparent reason, an old waster called Peadar had to be given a few lines to say at least once a week. This inexplicable requirement to write in Peadar was made more infuriating to the writers because the tight budget obliged them to use no more than four characters, Mrs Kennedy included, in any given instalment.

Marie Kean who played Mrs Kennedy earned a paltry two guineas per show, which was better than the going rate for the other actors who got a mere 30 shillings. The monetary reward for getting a few lines to say was poor, but, said Leonard: 'They fought for every farthing of it like wolves.' As the scriptwriter, he would have to decide who would earn a few bob for a bit part in any given week, and who wouldn't. This did not win him many friends amongst the cast of standbys. He remarked: 'The actors thought I hated them. Too bloody true.'

Despite the show's creative limitations, the characters came to be regarded as members of the family in households across Ireland. When President John F. Kennedy visited Ireland in 1963, he was reportedly asked in all innocence: 'Are you related to the Kennedys of Castleross?'

What could he say, but 'Yes'.

70: THE IRISH SWEEPS TICKET

Tormented by their law being made an ass, Britain's authorities imposed a blanket ban.

THERE IS A STRONG ARGUMENT to be made that during the middle decades of the 20th century the most instantly recognisable symbol of Ireland around the world was not the harp, or even the shamrock, but the Irish Hospitals Sweepstakes ticket. With its classically styled image of a young woman of noble bearing, its prominent serial number and its expensive watermark finish, the Sweeps ticket was deliberately and expertly designed to mimic the look and feel of a legal tender banknote.

In the autumn of 1930 the first of these tickets went on sale for an ambitious new venture which would take the world by storm. The Irish Hospitals Sweepstakes was the creation of three gamblers, Richard Duggan, Joe McGrath and Spencer Freeman, who incorporated themselves as Hospitals Trust Ltd. Their plan was to sell tickets into foreign territories, chiefly Britain and the United States, using Irish emigrant communities as their point of access and distribution. Ireland's crumbling hospitals were the token good cause. The promoters succeeded beyond their wildest dreams, despite the fact that their super-lottery was illegal in their target markets.

Hospitals Trust demanded, and got, light-touch financial regulation from successive governments. This was key because their enterprise relied on the bribery and corruption of police, customs, postal officials, ships' crews and politicians to grease the wheels of the biggest smuggling network on earth.

Relations between Britain and Ireland soured as British customs began searching passengers from Irish ships. This didn't stem the torrent of tickets arriving in suitcases with false compartments, in crates of laundry, and by other means. One large shipment was stuffed inside novelty plastic fish and transferred midway across the Irish Sea from an Irish fishing trawler to a Welsh one. Concealed in glutinous crates of real fish, the tickets were safely landed in a Welsh port.

In Britain, one magistrate was exposed as a big Sweeps winner only days after fining a businessman for selling tickets. Tormented by their law being made an ass, Britain's authorities imposed a blanket media ban on all mention of the Sweeps. Hospitals Trust retaliated by becoming the biggest advertiser with the fledgling Radio Luxembourg. Boasting the world's most powerful transmitter, Luxy beamed frothy Sweeps-sponsored shows into Britain where all radio advertising was forbidden.

The Sweeps were an instant sensation in the US too, where the dormant IRA network was revived to control and expand distribution. This alarmed Washington, as did the wholesale bribery of the US postal and customs services to turn a blind eye to smuggling. Hospitals Trust even bought off US Postmaster General Jim Farley, who declared he did not see much point in enforcing an outdated puritan prohibition on carrying gambling material in the mail. For years after his retirement Farley would holiday in Ireland where he was given the red carpet treatment by his secret backers.

Many amongst the millions sending to Dublin to order tickets couldn't have identified Ireland on a map of the British Isles, never mind the world. Others didn't have the foggiest as to what the Sweeps even were. One African chief sent a postal order and strip of material cut from his Sunday coat. He requested 'three talismans' by return. These talismans should grant him:

'That I will command respect on all my subjects to be loved by them. Also to gain respect with the government and much promotions in my State.

'To become wealthy on races, lotteries and sweeps, and to gain back all my heavy business losses.

'To gain back my house that was sold by auction.

'To protect me from all evil charms. To gain sound health and long life.'

He added: 'You offer one talisman free when buying three at a time. I wish you therefore to prepare that in the name of my wife to protect her also from all evil charms.'

Countless families went to war over who actually owned a winning ticket. In one case a wife who believed gambling to be a sin forced her sobbing husband to burn his winning ticket. On another occasion a 90-year-old heiress was turfed out of her Manhattan mansion clad in just her nightie by her snooty butler. The woman had signed her ticket in the name of her beloved pet dog. The dog died before the draw and the butler claimed the grieving woman had gifted him the ticket. The woman was already rolling in money, but she wasn't going to pass up on the prize of $140,000. The two argued and the butler kicked out his mistress. When the woman returned with several NYPD officers the butler was vacating the house with his baggage. By way of formally tendering his resignation he informed his employer that he'd flushed the winning ticket down the toilet.

The legalisation of gambling in the USA in the 1960s marked the beginning of a lingering death for the Sweeps, which finally closed in 1987. Despite the best efforts of the promoters to call in favours from their friends in Ireland's main political parties they failed to land the running of the new National Lottery which opened that year.

71: THE MASSEY FERGUSON TRACTOR

Remove the back wheels of your car and within the hour you have a handy tractor.

IN AUGUST 1910 A LARGE CROWD of curious spectators gathered at Leopardstown in south Dublin for Ireland's first air show. It was just seven years since Orville Wright had made the first 12-second manned flight at Kitty Hawk in North Carolina, and only a year since the world's first aviation jamboree in France.

Most of the flimsy aircraft were home made and consisted of a wooden frame covered in canvas with an engine capable of powering one of today's self-drive lawnmowers. The star of the show was the renowned motorcycle racer Harry 'Mad Mechanic' Ferguson who had made Ireland's first manned flight at Hillsborough, County Down, in December 1909, covering 130 metres.

Belfastman Ferguson found great celebrity with an invention that took to the skies for the first time in 1903, but he would make his reputation and his fortune with one that only got its name two years before that, the tractor. The first tractors recognisable as such to modern eyes appeared in the 1850s or 1860s, were mostly confined to road haulage, and went by several titles usually involving the term 'traction engine'. The strongest claim to coining the word 'tractor' can be traced to the US firm Hart-Parr, whose Hart-Parr No. 1, launched in 1901, is widely regarded as the first commercial farm tractor. In 1907 Irish-American Henry Ford launched his own make of tractor, which was soon being manufactured in Ireland.

Harry Ferguson, meanwhile, set up a company to sell cars and tractors in 1911, but he remained committed to building and flying aircraft until 1913, when he settled down to the responsibilities of married life (while continuing to race cars as a means of letting off steam). By then he'd had some brushes with death. Just weeks after his star turn at Leopardstown he had nearly lost his life when a gust of wind caught his flimsy craft high above a Derry beach and dashed him to the ground. He eventually recovered consciousness and, badly bleeding, staggered some distance alone to a hotel.

At the beginning of 1917 Harry Ferguson Ltd, with outlets in Dublin and Belfast, provided the first motor ploughing demonstration in the northeast and the furrows were deemed to be 'remarkably straight and of a uniform depth'.

That year he marketed an innovative contraption of his own design called the Eros Staude Mak-A-Tractor Attachment which hitched up to a Model T Ford. Prominent adverts invited farmers to 'Convert Your Ford Car Into An Efficient Tractor For £90'. To achieve the desired effect, all the farmer had to do was: 'Remove the back wheels of your Ford and within the hour you have a light handy tractor.'

Ferguson's eureka moment was to grasp that a tractor and the attached plough could be melded into a single unit through the magic of hydraulic power, allowing the driver to control the action of the attachments in tow. He began to register patents for his groundbreaking designs. Rejecting an offer to work as an employee of Henry Ford, he set up his own US plant, but the two men sealed a close working relationship based on a handshake.

Ferguson's commitment to his work pulsated with missionary zeal. In 1943 he reflected: 'Agriculture should have been the first industry to be modernised, not the last.' Together with Ford he came up with a new breed of tractor that greatly boosted Allied food production during the Second World War, but the relationship with the Ford Motors giant turned sour after Ford's death in 1947. Ferguson won a huge compensation package from Ford in 1952, but a merger he entered the following year with the Canadian Massey-Harris company brought more wrangling and more frustration.

One of Ireland's, and the world's, greatest pioneering inventors died of a drugs overdose in 1960. Ferguson had suffered from insomnia and depression and the coroner's court returned an open verdict.

72: WANDERLY WAGON

**Many letters were posted with Green Shield Stamps
affixed to the envelopes.**

LONG BEFORE HOLLYWOOD DIRECTOR Neil Jordan hit the
big time with his dark fairy-tale *The Company of Wolves*, there
was a talking dog named Judge. As the name suggested, Judge
was the rock of moral sense at the heart of the children's TV show
Wanderly Wagon, which first aired in September 1967. Although
Jordan scripted only one episode, the experience stayed with him to
the point that he recalled it four decades later while discussing his
hit show *The Borgias*.

In its own low-budget way, *Wanderly Wagon* was as imaginative
as any of Jordan's dreamlike movies. Apart from its talking dog, it
had a flying sweetshop, a lippy crow, a fox who thought he was a
Chicago gangster, several Moon mice, and a roving brief that could
take the magic caravan from the ocean floor to outer space.

In late 1968 an advert appeared in the Lost & Found classified
columns of the national press. It read: 'Lost. Magic wand with a star
on the end which makes things disappear. First noticed missing last
week in the land of the Big Runner Beans. Please contact Rory,
O'Brien, Godmother, Judge, Grainne or Forty Coats at Wanderly
Wagon c/o Raidió Teilifís Éireann, Donnybrook, Dublin 4.'

The advert was hardly necessary. After a year on air *Wanderly
Wagon* was already receiving sacks of fan mail each week from

besotted and bewitched children everywhere. In a 1972 interview, puppeteer Eugene Lambert revealed that many missives got through despite the lack of a proper stamp. In some cases the young sender had simply drawn a stamp on the envelope, while many more stuck on Green Shield trading stamps.

On more than one occasion the Wagon wandered into the prickly parallel world of true life. In August 1969 violence flared in Northern Ireland in what became known as The Battle of the Bogside. The confrontation between nationalists, loyalists and the police was one of the triggers for the Troubles. Three weeks later, to the general acclaim of the parents of the Republic, members of the *Wanderly Wagon* cast travelled to Derry to put on a charity concert for the children of the nationalist Bogside district.

Fifteen years later, in 1984, the outside world of realpolitik intruded again, although this time it was less welcome. At a Dublin press conference held by the Committee for the Rights of Travellers, a spokesperson denounced the show as 'racial' for depicting a Traveller character as less than upstanding.

Wanderly Wagon reached the end of the road in 1982. A decade later it was fondly remembered in an instalment of the *Lifetimes* TV series, although some memories fell short of fond. Viewers were shocked to learn that Padraig, the faithful horse they'd adored as children, had died of colic around the time the first episode was aired. Sensitive to the impact this may have had on young minds, the cast and crew circled the wagons and the tragic loss was hushed up.

Another unpalatable truth to emerge was that the wagon itself was no dream-mobile populated by cuddly talking animals. For the 15 years it stood parked at RTÉ's Montrose headquarters it was a dank, smelly empty shell used as an ashtray-cum-dustbin by station staff who littered the floor ankle-deep with cigarette butts and sweet wrappers.

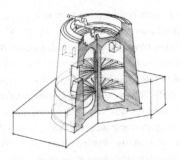

73 THE MARTELLO TOWER

Joyce moved out, disturbed by the late-night horseplay of his host and another guest involving a revolver.

CONTRARY TO A WIDESPREAD POPULAR BELIEF, the Martello tower is not unique to Ireland. While around 50 were built on the island, mostly flanking Dublin, running north along the east coast to Drogheda and south to Bray, more than double that number were constructed in the south of England and the Channel Islands. Based on the design of a protective tower constructed on Corsica's Mortella Point (hence the name) in 1565, they were built to defend the British Isles against attack and invasion by Napoleon's French fleet in the early 1800s.

Two floors high and garrisoned by around 20 men, the towers were built with thick cannonball-proof walls and a flat roof which allowed a single heavy canon a complete 360° firing circle. They proved so effective in defence and attack that examples can still be found standing in the United States, Canada, Africa and across the Caribbean. One of several towers constructed in Bermuda was on the tiny island of Ireland.

The last Martello tower ever built was erected in 1857 at Fort Denison in Australia's Sydney Harbour, and today stands as a museum, just a stone's throw from Sydney Opera House. Work had begun on the tower years earlier but had been abandoned when the prospect of attack abated. That threat returned during the Crimean

War when the British believed that there was a good chance the Russians would invade Sydney.

Australia's lone Martello tower, and indeed Sydney Harbour itself, had been originally commissioned more than two decades earlier by Dubliner Richard Bourke in his capacity as Governor of New South Wales. The cousin of the great philosopher Edmund Burke, Richard Bourke was a mixed bag if judged on a scale of 21st-century political correctness. In 1835 he issued a proclamation which stands as one of the key documents in Australian history, green-lighting the British colonial doctrine of *terra nullius* which stated that the land belonged to no one before the Crown showed up to take possession. Bourke's proclamation was the permission slip for a giant land-grab from the aboriginal inhabitants of 40,000 years.

A monstrous enforcer in terms of race relations, Bourke was an enlightened moderniser when it came to integrating transported ex-cons into civil society, curbing the excesses of hanging judges, policing protocols of religious equality amongst the Christian Churches, and clamping down on expenses scams amongst public servants. In 1837 he named Victoria's state capital Melbourne, after the British Prime Minister of the day.

Arguably the most famous Martello tower in the world today is the one in the Sandycove neighbourhood of Dublin Bay that bears the name of James Joyce. The author is thought to have stayed over as a guest there for as few as six nights in 1904, but he channelled the visit into the opening scene of the most talked-about novel of the 20th century, *Ulysses*. The aimless wanderings of Stephen Dedalus, which give the novel much of its structure, arise from his decision not to return to the tower after breakfast following a falling-out with the official tenant, Buck Mulligan.

Mulligan was based on the distinguished sportsman, medic and writer Oliver St John Gogarty, whose wide-ranging lifetime achievements would include a short footballing career with Preston North End, a stint as one of Ireland's top cyclists (before ungentlemanly language on the track earned him a ban), and a bronze medal for poetry at the 1924 Paris Olympics.

In a letter to a friend, Gogarty revealed that he had rented the Martello Tower specifically to 'house the Bard', meaning Joyce, who as ever was strapped for cash and needed 'a year in which to finish his novel'. Bad blood between the two men appears to have stopped Joyce from moving in as scheduled, and when he did eventually arrive he made his excuses and left at the first opportunity. Many years later Gogarty wrote that Joyce had moved out, disturbed by the late night horseplay of his host and another guest involving a revolver.

74: THE CATTLE BOAT

Concerned questions were tabled in the Dáil under the heading 'Emigration of Girls'.

IN 1951, IN A DEEPLY Freudian typographical error, the *Evening Herald* reported the findings of 'the biggest census of copulation ever taken in the State'. The latest population survey recorded that tens of thousands of mostly young Irish people were emigrating each year to work in British factories and hospitals, and to labour rebuilding cities bombed to rubble by the Nazis.

For successive generations forced to leave for Britain in search of a living wage, the only means of passage was to bunk in with the heavy traffic of beef on the hoof crossing the Irish Sea every day. Strictly no-frills, these crossings were an endurance test on the best of days. When the seas turned rough they were nightmarish, with seasick passengers tossed about ankle deep in a swill of spilt drink and vomit. Many men blotted out the ordeal with drink, an option generally not open to young women in an age when convention frowned upon such behaviour.

Concerned questions were tabled in the Dáil in 1951 under the heading 'Emigration of Girls'. But the concerns had nothing to do with the dismal conditions on the cattle boats. As was usual, the cause of worry was moral corruption. One deputy suggested that young Irish girls were being lured under false pretences to England, where they were being led off the straight and narrow to endure a fate worse than death.

He asked the Minister 'if his attention has been drawn to advertisements appearing in the Irish daily newspapers specially drawn up for the purpose of encouraging the emigration of young Irish girls to Britain as student nurses; and whether, in view of the dishonest nature of many of these advertisements, he will cause the Government to take such steps as are necessary to prohibit their continued publication'. The Minister replied that there was no evidence that the adverts for nurses and domestics had any evil intent, and that he did not have the legal authority to ban them anyway.

In that year of 1951 the Irish civil service finally completed a study of 'incidents of immorality' amongst the mostly young folk swarming to Britain. The document reported: 'A Catholic welfare officer stated that from her experience 75 per cent of Irish girls becoming pregnant do so by Irish boys. A barman had three children by different Irish girls.' Most shocking of all though: 'Another Irish girl living with a coloured man had a baby by him.' The study related several scare stories of Irish girls having their babies adopted by non-Catholic families.

The government report cited many instances of married Irish men going to England 'in good faith' to seek work. However, it said that the men would then often drop out of contact with their families, and that some wives back in Ireland were resorting in desperation to applying for a police warrant to have their husbands tracked down and hauled back to them. However, some deserted wives didn't see the police as an option. The report said: 'Many of their wives, fearing scandal and gossip in Ireland, are reluctant to approach the police, and write to priests [in Britain], hoping something can be done. Most of these men are to be found living with some other woman.'

The Reverend T. T. Dinan, an Irish priest based in Birmingham, told of Irish construction workers sleeping 'in relays' because they had access to their beds and tiny flats only on a timeshare basis. The cleric lamented: 'They have no home life and are forced to spend their leisure in dance halls and public houses where they meet bad characters.' Irish journalists following up the story reported back from England that Irish workers over there had to endure living conditions only slightly better than those of 'the negro'.

Taoiseach Éamon de Valera responded with a call to Ireland's economic exiles living, he said, in 'absolute degradation' to come home to a better life in Ireland. The results of the next census appeared to prove conclusively that there were no takers for his proposition.

75: CLERY'S CLOCK

The huge plate-glass windows ran molten into the channel from the terrific heat.

'I'LL MEET YOU UNDER CLERY'S CLOCK' entered the capital city's lexicon in the days when the city's horse-drawn trams would converge outside O'Connell Street's famous department store. Clery's timepiece has been a landmark meeting spot for generations of courting couples, country cousins and foreign visitors. The 21st-century incarnation of the clock dates only from 1990, although Dubliners have been shopping at the same spot for over 200 years.

In 1852 five drapers' stores standing in a row on Sackville Street, as it was then known, were knocked down to make way for Dublin's much-hyped new tourist attraction, the Palatial Mart, or New Mart.

The Palatial Mart, which opened its doors in May 1853, was built to impress. Not only was it one of the first purpose-built department stores in the world, it was so huge and its massive plate-glass windows so dazzling that foreign newspapers ran gushing reports of the spectacle.

The store was not for the hoi polloi. It catered exclusively to the upper classes and most customers would order goods for home delivery and settle their accounts on a monthly basis. One of the store's early adverts promoted a sale – or a 'Great Sacrifice' – of Wellington Boots. Recently laid to rest, the victor of Waterloo who gave his name to the footwear was a Dubliner, and his high-ranking family members still calling Dublin their home were the class of valued customer the store pursued. The Palatial Mart was renamed Clery's in 1883 when it was bought by M. J. Clery of Limerick. During the 1916 Rising, rebel Oscar Traynor saw the building go up in flames that were intensified by vats of turpentine exploding in the hardware store next door. He wrote: 'I had the extraordinary experience of seeing the huge plate-glass windows run molten into the channel from the terrific heat.'

The store rose from the ashes in 1922, emerging into a cash-strapped independent Ireland and a changed retail world. The market for luxuries from Paris had shrunk severely. Clery's went to the wall in 1941 and arch-rival Denis Guiney bought it from receivership, pitching it resolutely at rural Middle Ireland. The bywords of the new Clery's were affordability and durability.

Early on, Guiney came up with the brainwave of offering to refund shoppers their train fare if they spent more than £5 in the store. It was an inspired ploy, and by the dawn of the 1960s Clery's clock was arguably the country's best-known landmark after Nelson's Pillar, which towered just outside its front door until felled by an IRA freelance bomber in 1966.

76: THE SHOVEL

One driver made a round trip from Cork to Monaghan to roll a bog road, taking nine days there and nine days back.

I F THE ROADS TO NOWHERE forged in blood, sweat and tears during the Great Famine became notorious emblems of a nation on its knees, the ones that today form the vital arteries of Britain, America, Australia and other lands signify the resurrection that followed.

The terms 'Irish' and 'Navvy' have become joined at the hip in the lexicon of road building, but the term 'navvy' was actually coined in England during the canal-building boom of the early Industrial Revolution when the new man-made waterways were also known as 'navigations'. Published in the early 1980s, a study of census records by historian David Brooke established beyond doubt that the vast majority of navvies in 19th century Britain were English, but he added that 'only the ubiquitous Irish can be regarded as a truly international force in railway construction'.

Indeed, the Irish navvy was already a truly international force before the flight from the famine-stricken land after the 1840s. As Ireland's fragile potato economy began to groan under the weight of a huge population explosion, tens of thousands shipped off to the United States between 1817 and 1825 to labour on the Erie Canal linking the Atlantic to the Great Lakes via New York. As the giant Erie Canal project was finishing up, the first railroad companies in the States were being set up, and these epic schemes would soon lure entire armies of labourers from Ireland.

No sooner had the railways replaced the canals as the fastest and cheapest means of transporting heavy loads than the internal combustion engine came along and roads became the way of the future. Again, the Irish navvy was in high demand. The early motor vehicles arrived into a world of rough routes laid for carriages and churned up by horses. Neither the internal combustion engine nor the motor-car suspension systems of the day were made to take the relentless pounding meted out by roads that were often no better than dirt tracks.

When the cry went out for smoother roads the world's largest deposit of naturally occurring asphalt was sitting idly by on the British-run island of Trinidad, just waiting to be put to some good use.

Columbus landed on Trinidad in 1498 and the Spaniards colonised the island in 1532, but it was an enemy charting the lie of the land, Sir Walter Raleigh, who first recorded the vast tar basin known as Pitch Lake in 1595. A resident of Cork and former Mayor of Youghal, Raleigh marvelled at the tar in such abundance, and wrote in his diary that he used 'stone pitch' for caulking (sealing) the seams of his ships, declaring the sticky black tar to be 'most excellent good'.

Britain seized Trinidad from the Spanish in 1797 and while the pitch from the lake was put to a variety of local uses, it would be half a century before someone recognised it as a great resource ripe for the exploitation.

That someone was Admiral Thomas Cochrane, Earl of Dundonald. In 1851 the visionary seaman took out a patent to use the lake asphalt for 'improvements in the construction and manufacture of sewers, drains, waterways, pipes, reservoirs and receptacles for liquids or solids, and for the making of columns, pillars, capitals, pedestals, bases and other useful and ornamental objects, from a substance never heretofore employed for such manufactures'.

With those far-seeing patents, Dundonald laid the foundations not just for a new industry, but for the coming age of the motor car. It would be a few more decades before the demand caught up with the supply but, with the arrival of the age of the car, asphalt became one of the key natural resources of the 20th century.

As the newly independent Irish Free State began repairing and expanding a crumbling road system damaged further by the War of Independence and the Civil War, an elevated new form of navvy appeared – the roller driver. In 1913 the South of Ireland Asphalt Company (SIAC) laid the first example of rolled asphalt road surfacing in Ireland. From the outset, the steamroller drivers were the star performers of the new company, taking home a bigger pay packet than their foremen. In those times low-loader trailers were yet to be thought of, so the roller drivers would set off on journeys by road which would often take days just to travel a few miles. One driver made a 360-mile round trip from Cork to County Monaghan to roll a bog road, taking nine days there and nine days back at 20 miles per day. In tow behind the steamroller was a van for eating and sleeping, a water cart, a dog kennel for his guard dog, and, to keep him supplied with fresh eggs, a chicken coop with hen.

77: THE MASS CARD

Canon law forbade the acceptance of bribes for going soft in confession, specifically for letting the penitent off with mortal sins.

PRAYER CARDS OR HOLY CARDS have been part of Catholic religious observance in Ireland and elsewhere for generations. In or around the size of a playing card, they typically feature the image of Jesus, Mary, the Holy Spirit or a saint on one side, with the words of a prayer on the flip. Some cards profess to grant an indulgence to the person who recites the printed prayer.

A variation, the Mass card, has long been a popular way in Ireland of expressing condolences to a bereaved family. The idea is that the card is completed with the name of the deceased and then signed by a priest who undertakes to say a special Mass for the soul of the departed. In 2014 the average price of a Mass card purchased over the counter or online was €5 to €6 plus VAT.

In Catholic theology, an indulgence (from the Latin for offering kindness or tenderness) is usually defined as 'a remission of the temporal punishment due to sin, the guilt of which has been forgiven'. However, the precise meaning of this ethereal thing is so difficult to nail down that one online Catholic encyclopaedia begins its attempted definition with a section entitled 'What An Indulgence Is Not'.

The sale of indulgences by Catholic clerics to Europe's laity was one of the chief causes of the Protestant Reformation. While individuals like Martin Luther were concerned that the practice was spiritually corrupt, the northern European princes and nobles who supported the revolt were generally more upset by the huge drain of ready cash literally going south from their fiefdoms to the coffers of the Vatican.

Named after Simon Magus, the most glamorous of the many miracle workers who rivalled Jesus for the ear of the general public, simony is the sin of paying your way up the Church ladder or selling spiritual favours. The extent to which the medieval Church was riddled with bribery and corruption can be gauged by the wide range of canon laws drafted forbidding the sale of tithes, the charging of fees to administer sacraments, and accepting bribes to go soft in confession, specifically where this involved letting sinners off with mortal sins.

The Pardoner is one of several pious charlatans lampooned by Chaucer in his *Canterbury Tales* which exposed a Church in deep disrepute over a century before Martin Luther decided to take matters into his own hands. Pardoners would travel the land selling pardons, often in the form of written indulgences, to sinners who generally couldn't read. Sales of indulgences for the dead, the medieval equivalent of the Mass card, were a huge earner, and the salesmen often didn't let the small detail of religious orthodoxy get in the way. Some claimed that for a small fee they could arrange for the souls of the damned to be sprung from Hell.

In 2009 the Catholic Church found itself in a legal dispute with one of Ireland's biggest importers of Mass cards. The individual in question was Thomas McNally, a merchant of Longford town whose commercial activities included the import of Mass cards for over-the-counter sale in what he described as a 'highly competitive' business. The Catholic Church opposed the sale of cards pre-signed in bulk and often imported from dubious sources in Africa, South America and elsewhere.

Shortly before the dispute went public, Bishop Michael Smith of Meath charged: 'These cards have no spiritual value. They trade on the faith and goodwill of people.' The Church claimed that Catholics buying these mass-produced cards had no way of knowing if the pre-paid Mass would ever be said. It pointed out that one series of 120,000 cards sold wholesale by McNally in Ireland in 2009 bore the signature of one Fr Oscar Mkondana, who had been suspended by his bishop in 2003, and another of Fr Martin Njoroge of Kenya, who was murdered that same year. McNally countered that although Fr Mkondana had been suspended, he was still able to say Mass in private.

Finding in favour of the provisions of the 2009 Charities Act, which outlawed the sale of the cards without permission from the Irish Catholic Church, the judge held that there was ample evidence to show that certain businesses activities could mislead ordinary purchasers as to the authenticity of their Mass Cards and their compliance with canon law. The judge added that the payments made by McNally's company to priests for celebrating Masses for the dead was 'surprising', as it amounted to only 'a tiny fraction' of the sales turnover.

78: THE MUSICAL BUS

People from what property experts call the better
areas escape compulsory music on their journeys.

I N THE SPRING OF 1976 the company running Dublin's
public transport unveiled the latest breakthrough in in-transit
entertainment, the Musical Bus. In an age well before the first
Walkman appeared, the capital's bus passengers would now be able
to enjoy a selection of MOR pop tunes peppered with adverts
whether they wanted to or not, as they languished at some midway
point on their commute waiting for their driver and conductor to
pop back out of the bookies.

The mix of music and adverts would be piped to the top decks
of some 50 buses on cross-city routes. Reporting that the routes
had been carefully chosen, *The Irish Times* noted that these were
ones where 'it was thought the music might be more acceptable,
or where there might be the least objection'. Or, put another way:
'People from what property experts call the better areas often escape
compulsory music on their journeys.'

According to the same report, the thinking of the marketeers
was that restricting the blare to the upper deck would target the
youth, who preferred the upstairs seats. It was additionally believed
that since those seated upstairs were already prepared to tolerate
cigarette smoke, they might be more open to music and advertising.

The paper's leader writer lambasted the scheme, describing
the blare of 'unsought electronic tapes' as irritating 'gimmickry'
when the bus service should be tackling the scandal of rogue buses,
with no number or destination on display, cruising past queues of

dismayed commuters. Timetables were a joke, and the state of the filthy fleet was 'deplorable, ugly and sometimes dangerous'.

When the scheme was announced commuters swamped the letters pages of the newspapers with protests. One, however, urged calm on the basis that the new technology was bound to provoke a series of strikes by bus drivers and conductors seeking either more pay for switching the music on and off, or the deployment of 'a travelling electrician with each bus'. In the unlikely event that a single note would ever reach the ears of its intended victims, the writer predicted: 'The vandals complete with flick-knives and black markers will very soon cut off the sound and write suitable commercials on the walls and ceilings.'

But the sonic bombardment did commence, and Dublin's musical buses ran into a political storm in the approach to the general election of 1977. In 1973 Fianna Fáil had called a snap election in order to disenfranchise 140,000 young voters about to come onto the electoral register who might have been looking to stir things up. The ploy failed, and the party lost office.

Now, in 1977, Fianna Fáil set about wooing that same youthful slice of the electorate. Reasoning that young people loved pop music, the party unveiled what Senator Eoin Ryan described as 'a very lovely song' with a rousing political message. 'Your Kind of Country' was performed by Colm C. T. Wilkinson, who had come to prominence playing Judas in the Gaiety production of *Jesus Christ Superstar*. That role, he claimed, had caused a rift with his pious mother. ('*Anyone* but Judas, she'd say.')

Fianna Fáil's recruiting song identified itself with young voters who knew the pain of going straight from the school bicycle shed to the dole queue. With the growl of a wounded lion, C. T. opened up: 'Three years of loneliness, that's what I've been through / When I left school I joined me mates and we all joined the queue.'

There was no question of the State broadcaster RTÉ playing the party-political 'Your Kind of Country', but the musical bus looked fair game.

It was too good to last. After just a few days, CIÉ management banned 'Your Kind of Country'. The company wouldn't give a reason, but Fianna Fáil were convinced that the ban had come down directly from the enemy Transport Minister, Tom Fitzpatrick.

Fianna Fáil complained that the bus service was not bound by any requirement for political balance and they had paid fair and square to have it aired as part of the commercial breaks. The party further pointed out that the lyrics made no reference at all to Fianna Fáil. There was, however, a clever subliminal link in the form of stickers on the buses bearing the legend 'Your Kind of Country'.

CIÉ insisted that both the song and the stickers had to go. Fianna Fáil protested that the party had been running sticker campaigns on the buses for 25 years. The company relented and decided it would continue to accept Fianna Fáil's cash for stickers. When the vote was in, Fianna Fáil regained power by the biggest landslide in the State's history.

Dublin's musical buses ran out of road in late 1980 when the contractors, Sound & Motion Ireland, went to the wall. Despite everything, CIÉ pronounced the experiment a great success, having generated a total revenue of around £20,000 over the four years of the scheme.

79: THE IRISH DONKEY

The animal commonly known as an ass, which corresponded to arse, was sanitised to 'donkey'.

APTURED IN GLORIOUS TECHNICOLOR on John Hinde postcards, and given a sprinkle of magic dust in Patricia Lynch's 1934 children's masterpiece *The Turf-Cutter's Donkey*, Ireland's special relationship with the world's favourite beast of burden seemed in the middle of the 20th century to have stretched back an eternity. But while the donkey has been working for human masters since it was domesticated from the wild ass breeds of Nubia and Somalia some 5,000 years ago, its time in Ireland has been very much shorter.

One theory as to how the donkey got its name suggests that it was called after its most common colour, brown or dun, the latter being the ancient Indo-European root of the modern Irish word for brown, *donn*. The 17th century was the age when post-Reformation puritanism swept Europe and the new colonies of North America, and it appears that during this time the animal commonly referred to as an ass, which corresponded to arse, was sanitised to 'donkey'. The descendants of the Pilgrim Fathers were particularly enthusiastic about cleaning up the language, substituting rooster for cock, and rabbit for the English coney and Irish *coinín*, which came too close for comfort to the rude word 'cunny'.

It took the domesticated donkey many centuries to spread from its original workplaces in Mesopotamia and Egypt to Ireland. Indeed, since Columbus landed donkeys on Hispaniola in 1495, it seems possible, although perhaps unlikely, that they set foot in the New World before they first arrived in Ireland. The earliest known reference to a donkey in Ireland dates only to 1642, where one was documented amongst the livestock at Maynooth Castle. Some historians suggest that the donkey did not become a fixture on the Irish landscape until the Napoleonic Wars of the early 1800s when the British authorities commandeered the horses of Ireland for the battlefield, transporting over donkeys to take their place.

In her 1969 book *The Irish Donkey*, Avril Swinfen advanced an argument that suggests that ending up in Ireland generally spelled bad news for light-coloured beasts. She wrote: 'White has never been a very popular colour in Ireland with cattle because they were less able to stand up to the rigours of the Irish climate, more susceptible to vermin and subject to a complaint called white heifer disease which caused them either to abort or fail to conceive. Since the ass was owned chiefly by country people, the prejudice against the white cow can be assumed to have extended to the white ass, so that the white asses, like white cattle, were most likely gelded if males and seldom bred from if females.'

80: THE 'I SHOT JR' WINDSCREEN STICKER

Dallas was blamed for corrupting youth, marriage breakdown and the decline of the Irish language.

AS IF IN DEFIANCE OF Ireland's gloomy, sunlight-starved climate, the must-have car accessory of the late 1970s was the windscreen visor. The motor equivalent of sunglasses perched on the forehead, these sticky strips sometimes came in plain beige. At the close of the decade many peeling examples lingered from the 1977 general election, still bearing the Fianna Fáil slogan 'Bring Back Jack' long after they'd served their purpose of getting Jack Lynch reinstated as Taoiseach.

Then, in the late spring of 1980, everything changed. Across the land the old windscreen strips were ripped out and replaced with new ones that, in tandem with CB radio, reflected the national love affair with ten-gallon hats, cowboy boots, speaking with a drawl and generally pretending to be American. For years to come no battered Ford Escort would rattle around rural Ireland without a windscreen sticker proclaiming I Shot JR.

The JR in question was JR Ewing, the evil oil baron played by Larry Hagman in the blockbuster US TV soap *Dallas*. In March 1980 JR was shot twice, but was he dead and who pulled the trigger? (It transpired that he *was* dead unless he would climb down on contract demands deemed extortionate by the producers.) The cliffhanger played out for the entire summer and autumn until all was revealed in November. The 83 million viewers who tuned in to the tell-all episode entitled 'Who Done It?' was the biggest audience in US TV history, making up 37 per cent of the entire population of 226 million. When the same episode was screened in Ireland the following month, the 1.8 million who tuned in represented a gigantic 60 per cent of the Republic's population.

By then, Ireland's *Dallas* industry had been running at full pelt for six months, as the shelves of corner shops were cleared of Pope John Paul II medallions, flags, clocks and statuettes left over from the previous year's Papal visit, to make way for I Shot JR T-shirts, baseball caps, scarves and badges. Part of the soundtrack of the summer was the US novelty hit 'Who Shot JR Ewing?' given a lightning-quick Irish makeover by Westmeath's Tom Allen under the alias TR Dallas. The singer would later acknowledge the part played by his manager with the immortal words: 'Donie Cassidy is the brainchild of my success.'

In the normal course of Irish political life, trends in popular culture tend to take a glacial time frame to register with those running the ship of State. *Dallas* was no ordinary TV show and such was its impact that the political classes seemed to grasp intuitively that they could speak to the plain people by shoehorning in a reference wherever it could be made to fit. The Labour Party leader Frank Cluskey was first to name-check Hagman's character in the Dáil chamber in November 1980, remarking of a recent murder that 'the whole episode could be compared with the question of who shot JR'.

Weeks later in the Upper House, Senator Rory Kiely suggested that the power of TV could be better harnessed 'for the promotion of Irish-made goods'. As proof of this power, Kiely cited a recent survey of Cork schoolchildren: 'When one child was asked who the Taoiseach was, he said JR.'

And they were off. Accusing the pharmaceutical sector of bribing general practitioners with exotic junkets and expensive gifts, a member of the Southern Health Board charged: 'This business is impersonal and ruthless in the pursuit of profit. JR Ewing of *Dallas* fame is the prototype and he has many understudies.'

A TV debate between bishops and politicians over the future of North/South relations was described as attracting the same 'close attention' as 'a *Dallas* showdown between JR Ewing and Cliff Barnes'. An opposition deputy accusing the government of failing to maintain fuel supplies was dismissed by the Minister as just 'wanting a slot on *Dallas*'.

The rotating Taoiseach Charles Haughey was repeatedly likened to the ruthless JR. In May 1981, for instance, the Fine Gael Chief

Whip Gerry L'Estrange asserted:'Both are obsessed with their public images, both behave irresponsibly where other people's money is concerned and both try to maintain the useless pretence that the houses they rule are not divided. [This was a clever reference to 'A House Divided', the episode which climaxed with JR's shooting.] But it would take an awful lot more than even JR at his scheming and plotting best to help this unfortunate country out of the mess in which it now finds itself.'

Having decided that the way to the voters' hearts was through their favourite soap, the politicians just wouldn't let it go. As late as 1986, in a debate on rising crime, Senator Jack Fitzsimons blamed *Dallas* for 'corrupting the youth of this country'. In between, the show featured (not in a good way) in debates on sex education, marriage breakdown, a crisis in the Irish Shipping company. In one 1983 Senate debate, *Dallas* was even held partly to blame for the decline of the Irish language.

By the mid-1990s it was all over and the Irish people could afford themselves a backwards chuckle at *Father Ted*'s menacing village idiot Tom in his splattered I Shot JR T-shirt. Ewing Oil's corporate takeover of the Irish psyche seemed like a daft daydream while taking a shower.

81: THE TOURIST BROCHURE

Their want of civilisation, shown both in their dress and mental culture, makes them a barbarous people.

THE FIRST TRAVEL WRITER to cover the people and places of Ireland in detail was Giraldus Cambrensis, also known as Gerald of Wales, who made two visits to the country in the

1180s. His guide, *The Topography of Ireland*, appeared not long after the Anglo-Norman invasion.

Giraldus warned prospective visitors that the native Irish were a rough lot, partly because they were 'not tenderly nursed from their birth, as others are'. He continued: 'Although they are richly endowed with the gifts of nature, their want of civilisation, shown both in their dress and mental culture makes them a barbarous people. For they wear but little woollen and nearly all they use is black, that being the colour of the sheep in all this country. Their clothes are also made after a barbarous fashion.'

Having deliberated over the Irish national character at length, Giraldus delivered his final verdict: 'This people then, is truly barbarous, being not only barbarous in their dress but suffering their hair and beards to grow enormously in an uncouth manner, just like the modern fashion recently introduced; indeed, all their habits are barbarisms. But habits are formed by mutual intercourse; and as these people inhabit a country so remote from the rest of the world and lying at its furthest extremity, forming as it were, another world, and are thus excluded from civilised nations, they learn nothing and practise nothing, but the barbarism in which they are born and bred and which sticks to them like a second nature. Whatever natural gifts they possess are excellent, in whatever requires industry they are worthless'.

Five hundred years and more later, *The Topography of Ireland* was still the standard guide by which many English people formed their impression of their neighbours to the west.

In the years following independence, having just thrown out the British, enterprising elements began working on the process of luring them back as tourists. Writing in a 1928 trade magazine, however, one catering figure despaired that the country lacked even the rudiments of a tourist infrastructure. He lamented: 'Easter generally brings us to the beginning of fine weather and people begin to spend more time out of doors. Motoring and cycling are responsible for tempting folks into the country for short trips, but in many directions there is no attempt made towards catering for the refreshment requirements of these tourists. On one hand there is the local hotel with its heavy unsuitable meals and high charges, and on the other, third-rate tearooms where minerals are served in pint tumblers half-an-inch thick and teas in gruesome cups.'

By the 1950s, with the recently built Shannon Airport bringing in an entirely new breed of free-spending American sightseer, the Tourist Board lost the run of itself in getting the most out of artistic licence. Entirely ignoring the fact that many of the roads, including main routes, were little better than potholed dirt tracks one brochure gushed: 'A network of fine tourist roads extends throughout the country. If the visitor should wonder at the excellence of a road in some isolated, sparsely populated beauty spot, the answer is that it was engineered expressly for the benefit of the fortunate tourist that passes that way.'

There was probably far more truth in another passage of the same pamphlet which advised: 'If during your tour, you happen to meet any problem or difficulty, don't worry, just ask the first person you meet and he or she will probably move heaven and earth to set you right.'

That was Ireland selling itself in the 1950s. Three decades on in the mid-1980s, the American carrier Delta Airlines appeared to be still selling the Ireland of the 1950s when it ran a major advertising campaign on the back of a slogan that declared: 'Faith and Begorra, there's no better way to begin an Irish fling than with O'Delta Airlines.'

82: THE HARP

Henry VIII cemented the harp's association with Ireland when he issued his first distinctly Irish coinage.

THE EARLIEST EXAMPLES of the harp, and its close cousin the lyre, have been found in the ruins of the city-state of Sumer which thrived some 3,500 years BC in present day Iraq. From the outset this sophisticated instrument was associated with royal courts and the harpist occupied an elevated position in ancient Celtic society. The one displayed in Dublin's Trinity College and known as the Trinity College Harp is one of only three medieval harps to survive in the world, but experts have dated it to the 14th century at the earliest, dismissing claims that it once belonged to the High King Brian Boru who lived three centuries earlier.

There are references to the harp as the insignia of the Kings of Ireland as early as the 13th century, but it was reactivated in 1542 by England's King Henry VIII when he replaced the Lordship of Ireland with his own Kingship of the realm.

Henry cemented the harp's association with Ireland in the same period when he issued his first distinctly Irish coinage. He decreed that one side should feature the arms of England and France (he claimed the French throne), and that the flip side should show the harp.

Henry's new groat and half-groat coins were minted to pay the Crown's troops, administrators and general expenses in Ireland. The reason Henry was anxious to mark the Irish currency as separate from the one circulating in England was that it was worth a fraction of the English equivalent. In the years shortly after Henry's death in 1547, while the Irish and English currencies shared names and denominations, the debased Irish coins were worth less than half the value of their English counterparts if they were melted down for their silver content.

State papers released in 2013 under the 30-year rule revealed that in 1983 the Irish State pulled back from registering the harp in all its aspects as the official insignia of Ireland. The office of the Attorney General recommended that the government should register a figure of the instrument facing both left and right with the World Intellectual Property Organisation (WIPO) to guard against image theft. The left-facing harp had been adopted by the newly independent Free State in 1922.

However, according to official documents, the government rejected the advice out of fear that Guinness might challenge the official claim on the right-facing harp, on the grounds that the brewery had been using that image as its commercial logo 'before the founding of the State'. The government turned to the patent agents Tomkins & Co for definitive advice, to be told that, as the rules stood: 'We do not consider that mirror images of the harp symbol could be notified to WIPO.' Even if the Irish State did succeed in registering a right-facing harp, the agency cautioned that this might just store up problems for the future, saying: 'It is possible that such notification could debar the registration by Guinness of their trademark in territories where they do not currently trade but may wish to do so in the foreseeable future.'

The State opted to keep to the left.

Three decades earlier, after Carlsberg barged into Ireland with a big advertising budget, Guinness bought a Dundalk brewery and launched Harp, not out of any enthusiasm for lager but as a spoiler against the arrival of any more fancy new imports. The advertising launch of Harp was timed to coincide with the opening of Teilifís Éireann in 1961. Sales peaked in the mid-1970s, with the iconic adverts making a star of future *'Allo 'Allo* actress Vikki Michelle as Sally O'Brien 'and the way she might look at you'.

In 2013 Harp lager launched an advertising campaign with the slogan, 'Look on the Harp side' which, under international copyright law, is to the left.

83: IRISH DANCING BROGUES

Irish dancing would succeed where the Blueshirts, the Blackshirts and Hitler's Brownshirts had failed.

THERE ARE VARIOUS THEORIES as to why many forms of Irish dancing require its performers to keep their arms rigid by their sides. One is that the itinerant dancing masters who travelled the land in the 18th and 19th centuries placed a great emphasis on posture, to the extent that they even made dancers hold heavy stones to weigh down their arms. Modern judges are known to vet young dancers before a competition to ensure that a parent hasn't sewn the sleeves of their dance uniform to the dress, a practice that has caused some unfortunate children to fall flat on their face with unfortunate dental consequences.

Another theory is that as the Catholic Church established itself as the parallel government of nationalist Ireland from the middle of the 19th century, the touchy-feely elements of the bawdier traditional style were banished in favour of a more chaste format. Another, which strains credibility, says that the natives developed the technique of moving only from the waist down so that if any British authority figure happened to be passing the window or half-door, the dancer would appear to be standing perfectly still. The final, infinitely more plausible explanation, is that a lot of dancing took place in tiny confined spaces packed with revellers, and that there was simply no room for flailing arms with the result that the dancers concentrated on augmenting the rhythm of the music with their fleetness of foot.

While male dancers would have cavorted in their working brogues, many women in rural Ireland went barefoot until the early part of the 20th century. The brogue was identified by its decorative perforations known as 'broguing', which allowed water to drain from the shoes after a trot across a bog. When more formal Irish dances and competitions came into official favour after the foundation of the Free State in the 1920s, the standard dancing uniform for men and women was called Sunday Best, which meant exactly what the name said. Around this period female dancers began donning customised Ghillie Brogues, or simply Gillies.

After securing power with a snap election victory in 1933, Éamon de Valera's Fianna Fáil set about extinguishing the hated Blueshirt movement, which aped Mussolini's fascist Blackshirts who'd ruled Italy as a dictatorship for a decade. In 1934 the government brought its Wearing of Uniform (Restriction) Bill before Parliament. The Bill sought to bar the Blueshirts from parading in their paramilitary uniforms, holding public meetings where, as the Justice Minister put it, 'bodies of men may be armed, in a certain way, with lethal weapons, cudgels and so on', and generally setting themselves up as an alternative to the State police force.

One Senator, Kathleen Browne from Wexford, argued that the Blueshirts were doing a great deal of good work in the community, with Irish dancing a key component of the movement's social policy. She told the Seanad: 'Apart from securing order at meetings, we have organised large numbers of social gatherings. I have attended dozens of social gatherings – dances and other social functions – and I have seen the lord and the peasant, the farm labourer and the farmer, the town worker and the business man dancing and amusing themselves together ... The Blueshirt movement is the first movement in history that has done that.'

Six decades later Irish dancing would succeed where the Blueshirts, the Blackshirts and Hitler's Brownshirts had failed, achieving world domination in the Frilly Shirts of *Riverdance*.

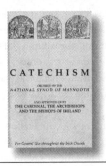

84: THE CATECHISM

'Such an instruction can tranquilize the adolescent.'

IN 1961, IN THE BEST INTERESTS of the young people of Ireland, Dublin's Archbishop John Charles McQuaid challenged the nation's doctors and psychologists to come up with a distinctly Irish way of telling youngsters about the birds and the bees without telling them too much. Naming 'the two greatest needs of adolescence' as 'temperance and fortitude', His Grace declared: 'I am convinced that there exists the duty to supply instruction in chastity that is accurate, clear, adequate and supernatural. And it can be done without hurt to sensitivity and without physical details.'

Properly formulated, he believed, 'such an instruction can tranquilize the adolescent'.

By the time they reached adolescence, however, many of the nation's children may already have been terrorised by the instructions they drew from their school catechism lessons, which were designed to be conducted in a call-and-response interplay between teacher and pupils.

The following are extracts from the long-serving *Catechism Ordered By The National Synod of Maynooth*, which carried the imprimatur of Gulielmus (William Walsh), Catholic Archbishop of Dublin from 1885 until his death in 1921.

Q: How many gods are there?
A: There is but one God, Who will reward the good and punish the wicked.

Q: How came we to be in the power of the devil?
A: We came to be in the power of the devil by the disobedience of our first parents in eating the forbidden fruit.

Q: Can anyone come out of hell?
A: No one can come out of hell, for out of hell there is no redemption.

Q: What is original sin?
A: Original sin is the sin we inherit from our first parents, and in which we were conceived and born children of wrath.

Q: Is it sinful to have unchaste thoughts?
A: Unchaste thoughts are always very dangerous and, when they are entertained deliberately and with pleasure, they defile the soul like criminal actions.

Q: What is matrimony?
A: Matrimony is a sacrament which gives peace to the husband and wife to live happy [sic] together, and to bring up their children in the fear and love of God.

85: THE FILM CENSOR'S CERTIFICATE

He installed mirror arcs to ensure he didn't miss any fringe glimpses of bared flesh on the margins.

IN 1927 THE COUNCIL OF IRISH BISHOPS, meeting at Maynooth, warned the people of Ireland: 'The Evil One is ever setting his snares for unwary feet. At the moment his traps for the innocent are chiefly the dance hall, the bad book, the indecent paper, the motion picture, the immodest fashion in female dress – all of which tend to destroy the virtuous characteristics of our race.' The following year in the *Irish Catholic Directory*, Archbishop Thomas Gilmartin of Tuam, County Galway, charged that 'bad pictures' finding their way into rural Ireland must take a large part of the blame for the fact that 'fashions bordering on indecency have become commonplace'.

By then, Ireland's home-style Prohibition Era was in full swing, with a clampdown on all things foreign and seductive, including jazz music, the English tabloid scandal sheets and the 'bad pictures' streaming non-stop from Hollywood.

Appointed in 1924, the Free State's first Film Censor, James Montgomery, worked tirelessly to turn back the tide of foreign filth. During his 16-year term in office he banned 1,750 films as against the 178 nixed by his British counterpart. Montgomery proudly boasted: 'I know nothing about films but I do know the Ten Commandments.' He may have known nothing about films, but he knew he was on the front line of a struggle by Church and State to control what the Irish people could see and think. The two largest parties, Cumann na nGaedheal (League of the Irish) and Fianna Fáil (Soldiers of Destiny) had both evolved from a puritanical Sinn

Féin movement described by one of its leaders, Kevin O'Higgins, with justification as 'probably the most conservative-minded revolutionaries' in history.

According to one modern-day authority: 'Montgomery understood cinema quite well and knew that he was powerless to some extent. He understood that he could cut out specific concrete things. He could cut out language, anything detrimental to the Catholic Church, bare legs and bare arms. But he understood that he could not cut out the dreamy, voluptuous awakening of the imagination that occurs when you are in a darkened room with the spectacle of picture and sound. He recognised there was nothing you could do to stop that, and he wrote that admission.'

In other words: 'He was a tyrant, but he wasn't a stupid tyrant. He recognised what was happening.'

James Montgomery may have acknowledged that he could not completely quash the dreamy, voluptuous awakening of the imagination that made the cinema such a magical refuge for the people of gloomy downtrodden Ireland, but he could do his best to throw blinkers on the spectator. As a key weapon in his war on what he termed 'monkey house morality', he installed mirror arcs to his viewing equipment to ensure he didn't miss any fringe glimpses of bared flesh on the margins of the silver screen.

He did his best to keep Ireland pure, but in his first report to government he outlined the difficulties of stopping the tide of 'indecent dancing' and 'the customs of the divorcing classes' which were the debased currency of Hollywood. He quipped rather wittily that: 'The real threat to Irish culture is not Anglicisation but Los Angelisation.'

Montgomery stepped down in 1940 at a time when the opening salvos of the Second World War were giving the censorship business a further shot in the arm.

Originally released in 1942 *Casablanca* was initially forbidden to Irish filmgoers on the ground that its anti-Nazi outcome was deemed to infringe Ireland's neutrality. Irish audiences were finally permitted to see the classic for the first time in 1946. When it was finally screened it was cut in such a way that no Irish viewer could possibly suspect that there was any romantic past between the characters played by Humphrey Bogart and Ingrid Bergman.

In 2005 the American Film Institute listed one of the closing lines from *Casablanca* amongst the 50 most memorable movie quotes of all time. It was 'We'll always have Paris', said with feeling by Bogart's Rick to Bergman's Isla as the star-crossed lovers part. But the censor's handiwork with his scissors had removed any hint that the couple had ever had Paris, leaving Irish audiences scratching their heads.

The key to the disappearance was that Isla was a married woman, and had been when she and Rick had had their fling in Paris. Even though she had legitimately thought that her husband was dead at the time, that did not absolve her sin in the eyes of Ireland's censor. She was still a married woman and it could not be shown that a married woman could have even an accidental encounter with another man.

Decades later, strenuous efforts were made to stop the Sixties swinging into Ireland. The acclaimed 1967 movie *The Graduate* hinges entirely on one pivotal scene where the experienced Mrs Robinson (Anne Bancroft) seduces the much younger Benjamin Braddock, played by Dustin Hoffman.

The seduction was the beating heart of the Oscar-winning movie, but it was ripped out for the greater good.

86: THE DE LOREAN

'I tell them to put the money into wine, women and song.'

WHEN HE GOT OUT AT THE TOP of General Motors in 1973, John DeLorean had the world at his feet. A gifted engineer and businessman, he had been the driving force in developing some of the most coveted so-called muscle cars ever built, including the Pontiac GTO, the Pontiac Firebrand and the Pontiac Grand Prix.

DeLorean struck out on his own with a plan to build the super-roadster to beat all super-roadsters. His first port of call was the government of Puerto Rico. DeLorean offered to establish his manufacturing plant there, in return for a large sum of seed capital from the Puerto Ricans. DeLorean pushed too hard and the deal fell through. Tentative talks about setting up in the Republic of Ireland also came to nothing.

As DeLorean's grand scheme seemed to be unravelling, the British government stepped in with a desperate gamble to ease the boiling sectarian tensions in Northern Ireland. The American was promised a huge chunk of taxpayers' money to build his factory in Dunmurry, just outside Belfast. The plant was to provide jobs in roughly equal proportions to the Catholics and Protestants in the sundered local community.

The stakes were high for John DeLorean. He'd ploughed his entire personal fortune of over $4 million into the venture, and persuaded superstar buddies including Johnny Carson and Sammy Davis Jnr to invest heavily. *The Wall Street Journal* gave short shrift to the razzle-dazzle start-up.

As the roof went on to the Belfast factory, the *Journal* noted that DeLorean was gambling his reputation and his fortune on what the rest of the US motor industry considered a long shot. It observed that his fabulous collection of classic cars 'has dwindled to a mere 25 vehicles' and that 'he has sold his interest in the San Diego Chargers football team but he still retains a chunk of the New York Yankees'.

While the financial bible said 'there is no way of knowing whether it will succeed', the report appeared to be pointing to just one conclusion. If DeLorean did manage to break into the cutthroat US market, his would be the first new major manufacturer to crash the big boys' club since the launch of Chrysler in 1925, and that was a big ask. The *Journal* also pointed out that the car due for launch on the US market some time in 1980 had been originally designed in 1975 for the 1978 market, so it was very likely to be the-year-before-last-year's model from the moment it appeared. And, at $12,000, it was already looking too expensive to compete, with the forecourt price destined to rise further by the time the first DeLoreans rolled off the Belfast factory floor.

A damning comment was supplied by Wall Street auto analyst David Healy, who said: 'When people ask my advice about investing in Mr DeLorean's venture, I tell them to put the money into wine, women and song. They'll get the same return and have more fun.'

As a cross-community experiment, the DeLorean project was no better than a sticking plaster solution to a society suffering deep internal haemorrhaging. On every other level it was a disaster. In June 1881, a year behind schedule and with John DeLorean's creditors battering at his door, the first batch of cars were turned over to the US motoring magazine *Car And Driver* for testing.

The verdicts were devastating. The testers concluded that every car had 'very serious quality problems' and fell 'abysmally short of any commercial standard of acceptability'. The magazine's technical director identified the biggest design fault as the distinctive gull-wing doors, where the fender didn't line up with the door, nor the door with the bonnet. The doors were so poorly aligned that they wouldn't close properly and in a couple of test scenarios the latch actually snapped. He pointed out that the first 500 vehicles which had by then been rolled out for commercial sale had been hastily pressed on prototype tooling instead of the required production-standard tooling.

Asked if these basic errors would scare off prospective American buyers, the man from *Car And Driver* confined himself to saying it would make them 'a bit more skeptical' before conceding that if DeLorean didn't buck up its product 'it runs the risk of being cast into oblivion within a very short time'.

And within a very short time the Belfast factory shut its doors for good. John DeLorean was arrested on charges of running a huge cocaine trafficking scheme in a desperate effort to keep his supercar dream alive. He would much later get off on a technicality.

And while the DeLorean DMC-12 (to give it its proper title) brought its maker to his knees, the car's faulty gull-wing doors would bring him the sort of immortality he craved, stealing the spotlight in Stephen Spielberg's 1985 blockbuster *Back To The Future*.

John DeLorean died from a stroke in 2005 at the age of 80. His tombstone features an image of the DMC-12 with the gull-wing doors at full span.

87: THE CREAM PHONE BOX

One popular method of stealing coins was to shove a baton of rolled-up newspaper up the B slot.

INDEPENDENT IRELAND'S FIRST TELEPHONE KIOSK was installed in May 1925 next to the Henry Grattan statue on Dublin's College Green. Prior to its unveiling, newspaper reports assured the public that these newfangled erections, which were expected to attract queues, would not be carbuncles on the face of Ireland's cities and towns. They would be built of 'reinforced concrete, with glazed panels, and designed so as to present a pleasing appearance and be in harmony with the surrounding buildings'.

Within a year phone boxes had become a feature of Dublin's railway stations, but the real boost came in the run-up to the biggest party in the life of the young independent state, which took place in 1932. In June that year the Free State hosted the Catholic Church's Eucharistic Congress to mark the 1,500th anniversary of AD 432, when Saint Patrick was said to have first come to Ireland. To prepare for the event 40,000 square yards of new road surface were laid in the capital and scores of phone boxes, newly painted in cream livery, popped up on the streets. The sight of all these mod cons going up in Dublin sparked a demand from cities and towns around the country for equal treatment.

The heyday of the Irish phone box spanned nearly five decades, from the 1930s to the 1970s. With a waiting list of up to five years to have a home phone installed, the phone box was as vital a public service as the bread man, the tinker or the moneylender. As Ireland got more phones there were more numbers to ring and by the 1970s the rain-sodden queues had grown long.

Once inside, the user was faced with a heavy black plastic dial-phone above a black metal coin-box and an empty wooden reading stand which had briefly propped up the phonebook before the latter was stolen as fuel for the fire. If the call was picked up at the other end, the caller pressed A to release the coins to allow him/her to speak. If the phone was not answered the caller pressed B for a refund. One popular method of stealing coins was to shove a baton of rolled-up newspaper up the B slot, converting the machine into a one-armed bandit. Alternatively, it was easy to make calls for free by tapping out the number, Morse code fashion, on the twin prongs upon which the earpiece rested.

Almost from the outset, robbing phone boxes became a family occupation for some of Dublin's inner city dwellers, with the tricks passed on from generation to generation. The cashboxes even attracted thieves from abroad. In 1938 Englishmen Fred Johnson and William Smith were charged with stealing money from a number of Dublin telephone kiosks. They were seen entering the public phone booths at Beresford Place, Ormond Quay and Botanic Road in Glasnevin. At Botanic Road they were arrested and found to be in possession of a penny coin which had been marked by a Detective Donegan. At the time of their arrest, both men had in their possession suspicious sums of coins in addition to the marked penny. One also had a skeleton key.

One garda gave evidence that he had searched Johnson's room on Parnell Square where he found a full kit of burglar's tools. He brought the case to Mountjoy Station and asked Johnson to open it. Johnson picked a steel file out of the case, removed his false teeth from his mouth and claimed he used the file on his dentures 'when my teeth hurt me'.

One later spate of thefts illustrated the astonishing versatility of the phone box. The original phone booths looked like Dr Who's TARDIS with a cream sheen. They were replaced by clear Perspex shells, which were prone to mysterious abductions. Two were erected in the Dublin suburb of Ballymun. When the engineers arrived the next day to connect them up, they were gone. Shortly after, a maintenance man at work in the Ballymun Flats discovered one of the missing phone boxes in a bathroom where it had been converted into a shower with the Telecom Éireann logo still on.

Killing time between pop-stardom and sainthood, Bob Geldof

fronted an early-1980s anti-vandalism campaign featuring kids chanting (to the tune of Pink Floyd's 'Another Brick In The Wall'): *We don't need your stupid messing / We all want to use the phone / Hey Stupid! Leave that phone alone.* With a scowl, Geldof slammed home the message: 'Phone wreckers are IDIOTS!'

Today, with phone boxes virtually a thing of the past, those idiots have kids of their own who don't even know what a phone wrecker is.

88: THE TILLEY LAMP

The ritual of pumping the base and lighting the gauze mantle became part of the daily routine.

FOR THOUSANDS OF YEARS the beaching of a whale on an Irish shore was greeted by the natives as manna from heaven. In addition to the food and fuel that could be salvaged from the giant carcass, the extracted whale oil burned long and bright in lamps, providing a coveted alternative to rush and tallow.

By the advent of the Victorian Age an expanding whaling industry was supplying oil for lamps on a commercial scale, and during the first quarter of the 20th century a substantial whaling fleet operated out of Blacksod Bay in Mayo. Between 1900 and 1925, 125 giant blue whales were harpooned off the Mayo coast, together with 600 fin whales and a smaller number of humpback, right, sei and sperm whales. As whale numbers tumbled, the business became unprofitable and the 1937 Whale Fisheries Act prohibited the hunting of baleen whales, a general name for filter feeders, in Irish waters.

By the time the Whale Fisheries Act was passed, a great number of Irish householders already relied on Tilley lamps to light their domestic homes, their farm outhouses and their way in the dark. During the First World War the English company started by John Tilley a century earlier began working with paraffin as a much safer alternative to the highly inflammable petrol lamps then coming to dominate the market.

In the 1920s the Tilley company moved into the manufacture of elegantly designed lamps which appealed to the house-proud owner, and for generations of Irish people the ritual of pumping the base and lighting the gauze mantle became part of the daily routine. The growing availability of electric light, and growing fears about the poisonous effects of paraffin fumes hit sales badly. The company relocated from England to Belfast in the 1960s before returning in 2000. Valued today more for their aesthetic appeal than their practical use, Tilley lamps have become valued collectables.

89: THE PARISH PUMP

The Irish Countrywomen's Association organised a Turn On The Tap exhibition.

THE PARISH PUMP HAS LONG SUFFERED a bad reputation through its association with sleeveen politics and the whole sorry business of public representatives putting the votes of the few above the needs of the many.

In fact, the coming of the parish pump represented a great leap forward for townsfolk and villagers across the land, who were spared the trek to the nearest well for drinking water, although many pumps were installed with a view to saving lives rather than long walks. The deadly waterborne disease cholera had been known in the Ganges Valley of India since ancient times, but with the opening up of new trades routes in the age of sail the pestilence suddenly swept across vast virgin territories. The second global pandemic reached Ireland in the 1830s and the third struck in 1848 at the height of the Great Famine.

With the population already weakened by disease and starvation, multitudes fell easy prey to the disease which flourished in water – particularly standing water – infected with the human, animal and vegetable waste that littered the stricken landscape. At the time no one knew how cholera spread. Most scientific minds subscribed to the Miasma Theory, attributing the spread of the disease to 'bad air'.

English medic John Snow discovered the link between cholera and bad water in 1854, just six years after it devastated Ireland, when he linked an outbreak in London's Soho district to a particular street pump. The water source for the pump was a well next to the Thames which bordered a leaking cesspit. Local officials removed the handle from the pump and the outbreak stopped, but the authorities initially refused to give credence to Snow's infected water theory because if they did, they would have to rethink and revamp the English capital's entire water and sanitation systems.

Whether Snow's ideas were accepted or rejected in Ireland, the post-Famine years sparked a construction boom in the erection of parish pumps. A list of busy Victorian pump manufacturers compiled by historian Brian T. McElherron included Tonge & Taggart with a foundry in Dublin's Windmill Lane, Dundalk's Park Street Foundry and the Dundalk Iron Works, and a Drogheda plumbing firm by the name of Branigan.

In addition to pumps funded by local authorities, some were provided to the community by the landed classes. One, endowed on the Limerick townland of Ahane by the Fitzgibbon family, was engraved: 'The pump placed on this spot by John, Earl of Clare KP, was renovated in 1875 and this memorial erected by his niece Lady Louisa Fitzgibbon of Mountshannon and by her husband the Honourable Gerald N. Fitzgibbon, in memory of their eldest son,

Charles Richard George, who died on the 30th July, 1870 in his 21st year. The Lord gave and the Lord hath taken away.'

A popular image survives in Irish folk memory of rural women in their headscarves gathered around the parish pump exchanging gossip until it was time for their husbands to come in for their tea. Insofar as this cliché had any basis in truth, it was a case of effect rather than cause.

From the moment there was the remotest chance of getting water piped straight into their homes, the vast majority of Irish housewives were ready, willing and anxious to do away with their regular treks to the pump to fill back-breaking containers. The ones standing in the way of such progress were the women's husbands. In the 1950s and 1960s the members of the Irish Farmers' Association vigorously opposed the direct supply of household water, fearful that it would increase the rateable valuation of their properties.

In 1961 the Irish Countrywomen's Association organised a Turn On The Tap exhibition at Dublin's Mansion House to support their case that the parish pump had had its day. It was a fight that in many cases would go on another two decades and more.

90: THE JACOB'S BISCUIT TIN

The infinitely versatile tin became a staple of buskers, beggars and politicians.

FOR OVER 150 YEARS the tin of Jacob's Biscuits has been the most enduring of all the gifts that are not just for Christmas. For years, and often decades, after the last biscuit has gone, the tin itself has enjoyed a long and useful afterlife as a versatile fixture of countless Irish homes where it could end up a thrift box in the kitchen, a toolbox in the garage or a store in the bedroom for love letters, old payslips and treasured trinkets.

Jacob's is one of the great Irish success stories. The firm was founded in Waterford by Quakers in 1851 to bake bread and make sea biscuits. The bread was good but the biscuits were better and instant success meant that production was moved to Dublin after just two years. The strides made by a factory set up in Liverpool in 1914 led to the establishment of a separate English-based company in 1922.

There were other smaller Irish biscuit makers, and imported brands, but such was Jacob's market dominance for a full century that they never needed to advertise. When Boland's Biscuits were launched in 1957 with a publicity drive to provide serious competition for the first time, the management at Jacob's were horrified at the notion the company might have to spend good money on the vulgar business of advertising.

Reluctantly, the company came up with a tiny budget for advertising, but the purse strings loosened after its two sponsored radio shows proved huge hits with the public. In association with Aer Lingus, *Come Fly With Me* flew host Harry Thuillier around the world to interview celebrities. But it was the *Women's Hour* agony aunt show with Frankie Byrne that really seared itself into the national psyche with its conspiratorial signature line: 'It's a programme for and, maybe, about you.' Byrne, who came to the job by way of the fact she was Jacob's publicist, weaved readers' dilemmas, her own frank answers and the songs of Frank Sinatra into compelling radio, and her shows became a keystone of the schedules.

Jacob's finally fully grasped the advertising nettle in the 1970s with the 'Who Is Jim Figgerty?' teaser campaign leading to the revelation that he was the fiendishly clever man who held the secret of how to put the figs in the Fig Rolls. Showbiz legend Maureen Potter was recruited to join some down-and-out relations of *The Muppets* for a sing-along rendition of every schoolkids' favourite jingle: 'Kimberly, Mikado and Coconut Cream – someone you love would love some, Mum.'

The infinitely versatile Jacob's biscuit tin, which was light to carry and broad enough to catch a lobbed coin, became a staple of buskers, beggars and politicians. During the 2002 general election one unseemly outbreak of political family feuding was widely reported as 'The Battle of The Biscuit Tins'. Fianna Fáil Deputy Beverly Cooper-Flynn was campaigning in Mayo having recently been found guilty in court of encouraging tax evasion during her previous life as a bank official. As polling day approached, she reached out to voters through the local press to remind them of the national media's 'very personal' reporting of the trial which had deliberately and systematically cast her in a bad light for doing the things she'd done. She said that the coverage was 'a terrible shame' and had upset her supporters to whom she offered her sympathy.

Those same supporters were visibly upset again when they attempted to take up a church-gate collection for the embattled TD, but found themselves fighting a turf war against fund-raisers for Beverley's party colleague, Deputy Tom Moffatt. Gardaí were called to break up the argy-bargy. Describing the belligerent parties as behaving like 'spoiled children', one observer told the media: 'The laughable thing is that there wouldn't be fifty euro to be got from the entire collection.' As the national media had a field day reporting The Battle of The Biscuit Tins, a Mayo police officer said Fianna Fáil's four candidates had agreed a pre-election roster for the holding of collections, but that one side had 'reneged' on the pact.

In 2009 Jacob's ceased the manufacture of biscuits in Ireland after 156 years.

91: THE MAP OF IRELAND

Petty called it the Down Survey because his findings were set down in map form.

THE FIRST GEOGRAPHER TO DESCRIBE Ireland's location on a map of the known, and often the imagined, world was the Greek astronomer and cartographer Ptolemy around the year AD 140. While Ptolemy's maps have not survived, his descriptions, accompanied by a matrix of coordinates featuring his revolutionary use of latitude and longitude, allowed medieval scholars to recreate his vision of the land mass that stretched from Ireland to China.

According to Ptolemy, one of the main settlements on the east coast of Ireland was called Eblana, and this was widely adopted in smart circles as a ritzy name for Dublin. However, scholarly research now suggests that Eblana probably referred to either the north Dublin inlet village of Loughshinny or nearby Drumanagh, which did a brisk import/export trade with Roman Britain.

The first scientific map of Ireland was surveyed by Sir William Petty between 1655 and 1656 in the wake of the Cromwellian re-conquest of the island. Petty called his exercise the Down Survey, apparently simply because his findings were set down in map form. The intent behind charting the lie of the land was to copper-fasten the massive confiscations of territory from those who had rebelled against the Roundhead Commonwealth in the 1640s. Petty shrugged off allegations that he had received massive bribes to take a creative approach to his boundary lines, and when the whole thing was over could colour in vast tracts of Kerry as his personal property.

92: THE PAPAL CROSS, PHOENIX PARK

Gifts included a canoe in Papal colours and cash from the 'cigarette allowances' of prisoners in Mountjoy Jail.

THE PAPAL CROSS USED AS AN EMBLEM of the Pope in ecclesiastical heraldry takes the form of a staff with three horizontal bars near the top. The towering white structure by the same name in Dublin's Phoenix Park has only one horizontal beam, but it was erected with full bona-fides for the first ever Papal visit to Ireland, made by John Paul II in 1979.

The Papal Mass beneath the Cross drew a vast multitude to the park on 29 September that year, with a great many enterprising souls granting themselves a special dispensation to serve both God and mammon for the day. With over a million people expected to start arriving at the Phoenix Park from 5 a.m., the faithful had been given advance warning that 'only invalids and the aged' would be provided with seats. In Cabra, one hardware store opened its doors at 5 a.m. with hundreds of fold-up chairs racked up on the footpath outside, bathed in light from the shop window. At £3.57 each the chairs cost a pretty penny, but it was going to be a long day standing in that big open field and they sold out in no time.

Inside the Park, the Mass-goers were directed to the cordoned-off corrals assigned to each parish. There they were easy prey for the armies of hawkers selling Mars Bars, cans of Coke and a huge range of Papal memorabilia. The Pope's face beamed out from cheap medallions, mirrors, brooches, album sleeves, posters, mugs and tea-towels, but in order to see the real thing the worshippers were urged to buy a cardboard periscope. Or, in the words of the hawkers: 'See the Pope for a pound!'

With the multitudes stuck in one place with nothing to do but wait, the newspaper vendors had a field day and quickly sold out to their captive market. Readers of *The Irish Press* learned that beneath the huge altar beside the Papal Cross there was a reception room where John Paul and a small coterie of guests would enjoy a buffet lunch catered by the Royal Hibernian Hotel. The menu featured 'salmon, oysters, crayfish, lobster, beef, lamb, ox-tongue and a selection of salads and desserts'.

The visit of the man born Karol Józef Wojtyla had a remarkable effect on Ireland's Polish community. When the Papal visit was announced a few short weeks earlier, newspaper reports estimated the number of Poles in the country at 'almost one hundred'. With the visit confirmed, a Dublin travel agent named Jan Kaminski quickly founded the Irish–Polish Society and the number declaring themselves either Polish or of Polish extraction shot up to 400. The Society had commissioned three gifts for the Pontiff, to be presented at the Papal Nunciature, which happened to be situated in the Phoenix Park, following the Mass. Gifts from other sections of Irish society included a canoe in Papal colours from the Irish Canoe Union and a cash collection from the 'cigarette allowances' of prisoners in Mountjoy Jail.

Days earlier, Kaminski and other members of the Society had convened at Dublin's Clarence Hotel to unveil the centrepiece of their presentation to the Pope. It was a piece of Waterford Crystal inscribed with a Polish eagle. The impending Papal visit had stoked the fires of the sectarian hatreds of the Troubles, and the Clarence event was disrupted when the bomb squad arrived to remove a suspect device planted in the basement.

Kaminski had been chosen to welcome the Pope to Ireland on behalf of the country's Polish community. On cue, he strode purposefully across the vast stage towards the Pontiff on the altar. Too purposefully for the twitchy security spooks. Years later he recalled: 'As I approached the Pope, they jumped on me. They clearly thought I was an assassin. I still have the press photos showing me in their grasp, gasping with shock.'

Those seconds of panic apart, it was a great day to be one of Ireland's 400 Poles, or one of the 20,000 from Britain's much larger community of Polish exiles who had arrived over for the event. John Paul joked: 'I always thought I had to go through Krakow to get to my home town, but now I realise I had to come to Dublin.'

Amid reports that the 400 would shortly gather for the first time to celebrate a traditional Polish Christmas, one delighted Pole remarked: 'The Polish community has just appeared out of nowhere.'

93: ROSARY BEADS

Hail Mary Full of Grace, Drink Your Pint And Leave This Place.

THERE ARE MANY CONFLICTING STORIES about the origins of the Rosary, the ritual sequence of prayers by which the Catholic faithful commemorate the divinity and life of Jesus.

One theory, much favoured amongst Irish Catholics, is that the Rosary evolved amongst Irish monks around AD 800 and was transmitted across continental Europe by roaming missionaries. A more widespread version is that the Rosary was a divine gift to Saint Dominic, the Spanish founder of the Dominican Order.

A thread common to many of the origin stories is that the Rosary began with communities of monks reciting the 150 Psalms of the Bible aloud. In most medieval monasteries the monks employed a large workforce of lay people to work the fields and do the chores, freeing the clerics for more spiritual pursuits. Listening in on these harmonious devotions, the lay folk wished to participate but they had no hope of memorising 150 psalms and less of ever learning to read them. So, the story goes, the plain people took to chanting one Our Father for every Psalm uttered by the monks.

From around the time of the Reformation, the Vatican encouraged the Catholic faithful to make a particular devotional link between the Rosary and the Virgin Mary. Devotees of the Marian shrine at Knock in County Mayo place significance on eyewitness testimony that when Mary appeared as a vision at Knock in 1879, she was holding a string of Rosary beads.

Not everyone accepted that testimony, however. In August 1979, in advance of the visit of Pope John Paul II to the Marian shrine at Knock, a newscaster on Irish television's main evening news informed viewers:'It's one hundred years since Our Lady appeared at Knock'. This statement of fact drew protests from a number of non-believers listening to the broadcast. RTÉ stopped short of issuing an apology. Instead, the national broadcaster offered the Jesuitical explanation that the newsreader's choice of words was intended as 'a courtesy which indicated the acknowledged recognition of Our Lady having visited'.

For generations of Catholic Irish families, the recital of a decade of the Rosary was the last act of the day before putting out the lights and retiring to bed. However, in 1928 the Irish Catholic Directory reported that the Rosary – and therefore the entire social order – was under threat. It quoted Thomas Gilmartin, the Archbishop of Tuam in County Galway, as saying: 'In recent years the dangerous occasions of sin have been multiplied. The old Irish dances have been discarded for foreign importations which, according to all accounts, lend themselves not so much to rhythm as to low sensuality. The actual hours of sleep have been turned into hours of debasing pleasure. Company-keeping under the stars of night has succeeded in too many places to the good old Irish custom of visiting, chatting and story-telling from one house to another, with the Rosary to bring all home in due time.'

The nightly Rosary enjoyed something of a comeback in 1954, which was declared the first official Marian Year in history by Pope Pius XII. The Pope decreed that the faithful around the world should revive devotion to the Mother of Christ through prayer initiatives, social gatherings, cultural events and charity works. In Ireland the 12 months of Marian devotion sparked a mini construction boom as the faithful erected shrines, statues and replicas of the Lourdes Grotto in parishes across the land.

By the late 1980s, however, it seemed that the plain people of Ireland were more interested in the new wave of British tabloids appearing on the newsstands with the word 'Irish' tacked on to the title. One, *The Irish Star*, drew attention to how far old standards had slipped, reporting on one Meath publican who was clearing his pub each night at closing time by playing a taped Rosary recital at deafening volume. The headline did nothing to uplift the tone of the report. It read: Hail Mary Full of Grace, Drink Your Pint And Leave This Place.

94: THE HURLEY

Both sides went at each other until their bones were broken and they fell outstretched on the turf.

MYTH HAS IT THAT the greatest hurler of all time was the Ulster warrior Setanta, who would later become Cuchulainn after killing a huge wolfhound with his hurley and a sliotar. A passage in the Book of Leinster says that as a child of just five years, Setanta 'went to the place of assembly where the youths were. There were thrice fifty youths led by Follomain Mac Conchobuir at their games on the green of Emain. The little boy went onto the playing field into their midst and caught the ball between his legs when they cast it ... Not one of the youths managed to get a grasp or a stroke or a blow or a shot at it. And he carried the ball away from them over the goal.'

The same annals, written in 1152, claimed that the very first hurling match took place two millennia earlier in 1272 BC. The game was a spur-of-the-moment thing, agreed between the native Fir Bolg and the invading Tuatha dé Danann while they were killing time before facing each other in the main event of the day, the Battle of Moytura.

The first hurling contest was a 27-a-side contest with no time limit and few rules. Both sides went at each other 'until their bones were broken and they fell outstretched on the turf and the match ended'. In place of the customary lap of honour, the victorious men of the Fir Bolg fell on their maimed opponents and slew them.

If the Irish annals are to be believed, the sport of hurling was already more than half a millennium old when the Ancient Greeks held their first Olympic Games in 776 BC. Hurling was contested at the modern Olympics for one glorious summer, in Saint Louis, Missouri, in 1904, but only as an unofficial sideshow with no medals up for grabs.

In 1924, 1928 and 1932 the Free State held its own Gaelic alternative to the Olympics, called the Tailteann Games. The modern games were touted as a revival of an ancient festival of sports held at the royal site at Tara, although dates for the origins of the games vary wildly from 1829 BC to 632 BC. At the last modern Tailteann Games in 1932 the hurling final was played out by teams representing Great Britain and South Africa. The game ended in a draw, but the judges were so pleased with the international cachet the two teams brought to hurling that they awarded a trophy to both.

95: THE IRISH WOLFHOUND

Cromwell issued an edict forbidding the further export of Irish Wolfhounds.

ESCRIBED AS THE LARGEST AND TALLEST of the galloping hounds, the Irish Wolfhound is thought to have arrived in Ireland along with, or shortly after, the first settlers around 9,000 years ago. Raised to hunt and guard, these short-lived giants (average lifespan is just seven years) were known as 'Cú' in ancient Ireland, and nobles and warriors would sometimes stick the prefix Cú at the start of their name to denote fierceness and loyalty. The most famous hero to do so was Setanta, who took the name Cuchulainn (the Hound of Culann) as a child after slaying the ferocious guard dog of the blacksmith Culann.

When the Anglo-Normans invaded Ireland in the 12th century they were immediately taken with the power, size and obedience of the Irish Wolfhound and they wasted no time in acquiring some for themselves. Court records show that in 1201 King John gave an order at Portsmouth that his Irish hounds be provided with suitable accommodation while later papers show his successors Edwards I and III taking possession of these prized animals.

Such was the demand from England and further afield that the domestic stock of wolfhounds was becoming depleted by the 17th century. In 1605 the scientist Dr Caius had the dogs in mind when he bemoaned: 'We Englishmen are marvellous greedy, gaping gluttons after novelties, and covetous cormorants of things that be seldom, rare, strange, and hard to get.'

After Cromwell crushed the rebellious natives in 1649–50, he set about deporting the natives to Hell, Connaught or Barbados, and planting their confiscated lands with English, Welsh and Scots Protestant settlers. Two of the top priorities for the new wave of planters were to wipe out the woodland cover where the evicted Irish could loiter with intent, and with them the wolves which were felt to be in some unholy pact with the wild Irish.

In 1652, anxious to give the settlers the best chance of defeating the Irish and their friends the wolves, Oliver Cromwell issued an edict forbidding the further export of Irish Wolfhounds. It said:

> Forasmuch as we are credibly informed that wolves doe much increase and destroy many cattle in several partes of this dominion, and that some of the enemie's party who have laid down arms, and have liberty to get beyond the sea, and others, do attempt to carry away several such great dogges, as are commonly called wolfe dogges, whereby the breed of them, which are useful for destroying of wolves would (if not prevented) speedily decay. These are therefore to prohibit all persons whatsoever from exporting any of the said dogges out of this dominion, and searchers and other officers of the customs, in the several partes and creekes of this dominion, are hereby strictly required to seize and make stopp of all such dogges, and deliver them either to the common huntsman appointed for the precinct where they are seized upon, or to the governor of the said precinct.

The campaign to exterminate the island's wolves went on for more than a century, until the last wolf in Ireland was reportedly brought down in 1786 in Myshall, County Carlow, by a pack of wolfhounds kept by a Mr Watson of Ballydarton.

96: THE SCHOOLBOOK

Even in the 1960s the Russian economy depends on
slave labour to balance its budget.

WHEN IRELAND'S NATIONAL SCHOOL SYSTEM was set
up in 1831, its brief was to 'unite in one system children
of different creeds'. The National Board was 'to look
with peculiar favour' on funding applications for schools jointly
managed by Catholics and Protestants. However, the main Christian
Churches lobbied strongly for a segregated education system. This
pressure was so effective that by the middle of the 19th century only
4 per cent of national schools were under mixed management.

In terms of the curriculum, the guiding principle was that
schools should offer 'combined moral and literary instruction'.
While the Board would decide the broad outline of this moral
and literary instruction, each religious body would determine the
detailed form and content of religious instruction in the schools
under its patronage.

By the start of the 20th century the Irish national education
system was fundamentally different from those elsewhere in the
United Kingdom. In England and Scotland parallel systems had
evolved, so that parents had a choice of sending their children to
denominational schools or ones controlled by the local secular
authority. In Ireland, the vast majority of schools, primary and
secondary, were in the hands of the religious.

One of the top priorities of the new Free State was to create
a distinctively Irish schooling system. In 1925 a committee was set
up, under the Chairmanship of the Rev. J. McKenna SJ, to review
the curriculum.

Amongst its findings, the committee's report stated: 'Of all the parts of the school curriculum Religious Instruction is by far the most important, as its subject matter, God's honour and service, includes the proper use of all man's faculties, and affords the most powerful inducements to their proper use. We assume therefore, that Religious Instruction is a fundamental part of the school course. Though the time allotted to it as a specific subject is necessarily short, a religious spirit should inform and vivify the whole work of the school.'

The new schoolbooks of Independent Ireland reflected this spirit. Published by the Christian Brothers in 1932, the *Senior Reader* for secondary schoolboys featured piles of poetry and essays such as 'A Frost Bitten Nose', 'The First Flight To The North Pole' and 'On Prayer'. In addition, many of the texts for reading aloud in English class were prayers.

The second text in the *Senior Reader* was entitled 'The Evils of Drink'. One passage for recital went: 'Is that thing that staggers and stumbles and reels and falls and rolls in the mud or lies helpless on the road – is that thing a man? ... What is it that has wiped out God's image and degraded him beneath the brute? It is drink, drink, drink.'

Another essay, entitled 'The National Ideal', made no bones about the fact that patriotism was next to Godliness, positing Christianity, the Irish language and a 32-county United Ireland as the Holy Trinity of the new era. It taught the message that: 'Like Christianity, nationality is a whole which cannot be tampered with, and which will not live in parts. Our National Ideal is an Ireland Gaelic in language and in character, an Ireland prosperous, whole and free. No part of this Ideal will live separated from the other ... Nationality without the language will never be recovered, and the language without nationality will never be maintained.'

Eight years later *The Rural Reader For Irish Schools Part 2* picked up the theme. In the book's introduction, entitled 'Farming Is Living', the Rev. J. J. Conway informed his young readers: 'Of three slender threads is our life woven. They are the golden thread of milk into the pail, the green thread of growing corn and the white thread of twisted wool. They are the true green, white and golden flag under which we live.' In fact, the citizens of the Free State lived under a green, white and orange flag, suggesting the author was uncomfortable with acknowledging the colour of the island's large Unionist population in a classroom setting.

This discomfort was reflected elsewhere in *The Rural Reader*, in the form of several sideswipes at 'the seed of Cromwell' and a passage in the chapter entitled 'The Land War Ends', which welcomed the ruin of 'the vast houses of the landlord caste now decaying in Dublin'. Ireland should rejoice to get shot of this part of its heritage because the big houses 'were built out of extractions from men of the old stock who drained, tilled and made the land to which, by rights, they were the heirs'.

The educators who commissioned and composed the new post-primary Civics course in 1967 saw the future very much as a steady continuation of the past. Their crystal ball certainly didn't tell them that inside of 20 years a popular movement led by an Englishman would desecrate one of the cardinal rules set out in Chapter 1 of the *Tomorrow's Citizen* textbook. Those Civics students who would become the future foot soldiers of Jack's Army must not have been paying attention when they were instructed that: 'The [tricolour] flag should never be used as a decoration, and letterings or pictures shall never appear on it.'

Under the section Custom & Law, tomorrow's citizens were told that: 'In the making of laws, men are bound by the law of God.' This message chimed nicely with the entire content of the chapter on Communism. Entitled 'The Reign of Terror', Section 2 began: 'We can only guess the number of people who were brutally murdered under the dictatorship of Lenin.'

Section 4, 'The Concentration Camp', opened with the line: 'Even in the 1960s the Russian economy depends on slave labour to balance its budget.'

And if any pupil was daydreaming of taking the emigrant trail to England in search of work, the section on Communism entitled 'Ireland' warned: 'Communism has made little or no progress in Ireland and its party membership is small. But because of the social problem of emigration, Irish people are particularly prone to the attractiveness of Communist Front organisers in Britain ... In Britain the Connolly Association has always denied that it is Communist ... It is in fact a "front" organisation for the Communist movement.'

Forewarned and forearmed, a great many of the pupils of the 1960s found they had no choice but to go anyway.

97: DANIEL O'CONNELL'S DUELLING PISTOL

The O'Connell family seemed to have a fatal attraction to the thrill of the duel.

WHEN DANIEL O'CONNELL DIED in Genoa in 1847 at the age of 71, Catholic Ireland mourned the passing of a saint, and in a manner befitting a saint his heart was buried in Rome while his body was laid to rest with great ceremony at Dublin's Glasnevin Cemetery.

But with the distance of time, scholars have come around to the view that there was much substance to the charges of his enemies during his lifetime that The Great Liberator led a double life as The Great Fornicator, and was an arrogant, violent spendthrift to boot.

O'Connell came to maturity in an age when the practice of duelling to the death was becoming increasingly frowned upon, but it continued to persist in Ireland even as it was being abandoned by British high society. Around the year 1800 the city of Dublin alone had 19 outlets making or selling duelling pistols, while some surveys suggest that the fatality rate in Irish duels was much higher than in the neighbouring island. The O'Connell family seemed to have a fatal attraction to the thrill of the duel.

In 1813 John O'Connell, the younger brother of Daniel, reportedly burst into a billiard room in Tralee and confronted one Richard Blennerhassett in a row over politics. His honour impugned, Blennerhassett demanded satisfaction and the pair faced off on a January morning. Both men missed with their first shot. According to newspaper reports: 'Mr Blennerhassett fired his second. The ball entered Mr O'Connell's mouth, knocking out two teeth, severely injuring his lower jaw and lodged in the back of his neck.'

Two years later Daniel O'Connell got into an argument with

Dublin Corporation over that body's treatment of Catholics. After O'Connell accused the Corporation of 'beggarly' behaviour he was challenged to a duel by a member of the Guild of Merchants, John D'Esterre. The two met at Bishopscourt near Naas in County Kildare where both fired at the same time. D'Esterre missed; O'Connell didn't, hitting his rival in the thigh. D'Esterre died days later, having reputedly said on his deathbed that he bore his killer no ill will.

In 1832 Daniel O'Connell's eldest son, Maurice, renewed hostilities with the Blennerhassetts after Arthur Blennerhassett had allegedly canvassed voters who had already pledged their support to the O'Connell camp. The two men met in combat after Maurice left a letter with Arthur's wife demanding a showdown with pistols at dawn. Both men shot and missed, and they left it at that.

98: THE BLARNEY STONE

To have ascended to it was considered as a proof of perseverance, courage and agility.

IT'S NOT MUCH TO LOOK AT, and it's not easy to smooch up to, but the Blarney Stone is one of the world's most famous slabs of rock. Roughly four feet long, one foot high and nine inches deep, the Stone is said to confer the gift of the gab on all who risk back strain and vertigo to kiss it.

The stone was set into the walls of Blarney Castle in County Cork in 1446 apparently above a sheer drop of some 120 feet. A protective rail has long been in place to prevent kissers from plummeting to their doom, although the facts are unsure as to when precisely these safeguards were installed. They were absent from the plot of the 1946 Sherlock Holmes episode entitled 'The Adventure of The Blarney Stone'. Starring the silver screen's classic pairing of Basil Rathbone and Nigel Bruce in the lead roles, the United States radio whodunnit featured a hated businessman who plummeted to his death while trying to win a £10 wager for kissing the Stone.

The risks attached to kissing the hanging rock are not confined to physical injury. The comedian Dave Allen made the point that: 'Only the Irish could persuade people to kiss a stone Norman soldiers had urinated on.'

Almost none of the legends surrounding the Stone bear much scrutiny. One involves the goddess Cliodhna, the Queen of the Banshees, who was asked for help by the builder of Blarney Castle, Cormac Laidir MacCarthy. Cormac was supposedly due in court to fight a lawsuit but feared he might fare badly before the judge. Cliodhna instructed him to kiss the first stone he found in the morning on his way to court, which he did, with the result that he pleaded his case with great eloquence and won. Delighted, MacCarthy incorporated the magical stone into a tower of his castle.

An alternative origin myth for the Blarney Stone is that it was a gift to the master of Blarney Castle from the grateful Scottish King Robert the Bruce in thanks for MacCarthy's support in vanquishing the English at the Battle of Bannockburn. Apart from the fact that the dates never matched up for this supposed gift giving, a 2013 study by geologists at Glasgow University revealed that the limestone that makes up the Blarney Stone is unique to the district surrounding the Castle.

Another legend has it that it wasn't Cormac Laidir MacCarthy who first kissed the stone on his way to fight a lawsuit, but a much later successor – Cormac Teige MacCarthy – who sought aid from an old woman as he set off for a potentially terminal audience with Queen Elizabeth I. Yet another improbable tale maintains that it was the Virgin Queen herself – irritated at MacCarthy's slippery plámásing – who coined the term 'blarney' to mean blather or waffle.

The Celtic Revival of the 18th and 19th centuries encouraged the foundation of the Gaelic Athletic Association and a renewed interest in ancient Irish lore. Along the way, it also produced the fanciful invention of several brand-new ancient legends. In his

1888 book *Ireland Under Coercion: The Diary of An American*, William Henry Hubert suggested that the legend of the Blarney Stone may have been at his time little more than a century old.

This seems somewhat doubtful as the term 'blarney' was by then well established in its modern sense. In his 1785 tome *A Classical Dictionary of The Vulgar Tongue*, Francis Grose penned the following entry: 'Blarney; he has licked the Blarney Stone; he deals in the wonderful or tips us the traveller. The Blarney Stone is a triangular stone on the very top of an ancient castle of that name in the county of Cork in Ireland, extremely difficult to access, so that to have ascended to it was considered as a proof of perseverance, courage and agility, whereof many are supposed to claim the honour who never achieved the adventure; and to tip the Blarney is figuratively used for telling a marvellous story, or falsity.'

99: THE PIONEER PIN

The Minister regretted that an unsavoury TV character was seen to wear one.

THE PIONEER TOTAL ABSTINENCE ASSOCIATION (PTAA) began life in Dublin's Gardiner Street in 1898, the brainchild of Fr James Cullen who pined for the 'Ireland Sober, Ireland Free' temperance rallies of Fr Theobald Mathew some 50 years earlier. At the time of that first meeting, Gardiner Street was at the sooty heart of Monto, the run-down red-light district where every second doorway led to a shebeen or a brothel. The sale of Pioneer Pins was key to funding the young Association.

Under Cullen's autocratic rule, the PTAA tapped into the Catholic Nationalist mood of the time and quickly attracted large numbers of converts to its lectures, alcohol-free dances, pilgrimages, prayer meetings and table quizzes. But for Cullen, the battle against the bottle was just stage one of his grand plan. He was mobilising a crusade to forge a better Irish society that would be pure of mind and spirit as God intended.

Schoolchildren aged around 12 were invited to take the pledge at their Confirmation, but the Association also put great store on cultivating membership and influence in key bodies like the GAA, political parties, the army, and the police. In 1922 the Free State's first Police Commissioner, Eoin O'Duffy, boasted that on a recent visit to a barrack in Longford, every single officer wore a Pioneer Pin on his uniform.

Politicians were quick to realise that the Pin provided them with an instant character reference. A report on the 1964 Fianna Fáil Ard Fheis began: 'Tweed-coated, Pioneer-Pinned, furred and chic, old and gnarled, young and svelte, fat, thin, bulbous-faced and wizened, sleek of mien and sharp in comment – there they were, the Fianna Fáil Party.' A few months earlier the Association had forced an expression of regret from the Minister for Posts & Telegraphs in the Dáil after an unsavoury character in a TV drama had been seen to wear a Pioneer Pin.

By mid-century, the crusade had helped create a strange partition in Irish society, much remarked upon by foreign visitors, where falling-down drunkenness and upstanding sobriety co-existed under an uneasy truce.

When 80,000 Pioneers brought Dublin to a standstill for the Association's Golden Jubilee in 1949, Ireland's most enthusiastic drinker Brian O'Nolan aka Flann O'Brien aka Myles na gCopaleen vented his spleen at what he saw as a bunch of Holy Joes flaunting their piety. He wrote:

> I can recall nothing comparable to yesterday's procedure and I hope somebody will examine the legality of it. If the abstainers are entitled to disrupt transport in their own peculiar and selfish interest, there is no reason in the world why the drinking men of Ireland should not demand and be given the same right.
>
> Let everybody stay at home because the boozers are in town! I would advise these Pioneer characters that there

is more in life than the bottle, that fair play to others is important and that temperance – taking the word in its big and general value – is a thing they might strive to cultivate a bit better.

Sadly a lack of temperance – taking the word in its small and specific Pioneer value – would speed one of Ireland's greatest writers to an early grave.

100: THE SHILLELAGH

A letter to Emon DeValery, Premier, Dublin, Ireland.

I N HIS THREE-VOLUME MEMOIR *Personal Sketches of His Own Times* published between 1827 and 1832, the learned judge Sir Jonah Barrington recalled various bouts of stick fighting he had witnessed during his eventful life. He wrote that they were 'like sword exercises and did not appear savage. Nobody was disfigured thereby, or rendered fit for a doctor. I never saw a bone broken or a dangerous contusion from what was called whacks of a shillelagh (which was never too heavy)'.

Forbidden to bear conventional arms by repressive laws of the 18th century, the native Irish took to carrying sticks, or *bataí*. These shillelaghs bore no resemblance to the stumpy cudgels sold to tourists, but were essentially sturdy walking sticks with a heavy knob on the handle usually formed from the root of the plant. A must-have accessory for participating in faction fights, the shillelagh took its name from the ancient oak forest at Shillelagh in County Wicklow, and while oak was a popular source of wood, the blackthorn walking stick had overtaken it in popularity by the turn of the 20th century.

In 1893, beneath the eye-catching headline 'Swallowed A Walking Stick', the *Evening Herald* reported on an inquest into the death of 65-year-old William Bolas. It read:

The deceased had been depressed. He was given a walking stick with which to knock the floor in case he required assistance. Nothing was heard of him during the night but in the morning he was groaning and was apparently in great pain. He told the landlady that he had swallowed the stick, and a piece of it could be perceived sticking out of his mouth. An attempt to abstract it was resented by the deceased who bit the young man's finger. A constable was fetched in, and he extracted one piece of stick which was 16 inches long. Deceased then commenced to vomit when another piece of stick became visible. The constable was about to pull it away when the deceased anticipated him and pulled it away himself. It proved to be 15 inches long.

The coroner recorded a verdict of death by suicide.

The National Archives in Dublin contain a letter sent from America in 1959 on a related subject. The missive arrived in the office of the Taoiseach addressed to: 'Emon DeValery, Premier, Dublin, Ireland.'

In it, Dennis F. Dunlavy from Ohio explained:

I have been confined to my bed for the past three months either at the hospital or convalescing at home, and I am practically learning to walk again. I thought perhaps you would have somebody engaged in the business of selling black thorn canes. My uncle had one with the thorns evenly around the stock about an inch or an inch-and-a-half through diameter. No doubt there are exporters who sell these canes and if you will have him bill me I will be very glad to make payment. I'm sorry to bother you, Your Eminence Premier, but I know no other way of making the approach.

The Taoiseach's Departmental Secretary informed Mr Dunlavy of Ohio that the highest office in the land was passing on his shopping order to the tourist authority Bord Fáilte.

101: THE FLAT CAP

He was hauled before his employers and told he had
better write his way out of trouble.

ROM THE MID-1960s to the end of the 1970s Ireland's most
famous man in a flat cap was the soap character Benjy Riordan
played by Tom Hickey. Set in the fictitious townland of
Leestown in County Kilkenny, *The Riordans* began life as an early
exercise in what would come to be labelled 'infotainment'. The
national broadcaster conceived the show as a vehicle for spreading
the word to the farming community about the latest developments in
growing techniques and machinery.

In the words of Gunnar Ruggheimer, Teilifis Éireann's Controller
of Programmes, the goal of the soap was 'to get across surreptitiously
ideas about good farm management and farm practices ... and to
make certain that the actual manipulation of farm equipment is in
accordance with normal practice. The whole validity of the series,
which of course is built on its verisimilitude to a real situation,
depends on the actors acting like farmers in every last situation.'

In order to capture the real-life workings of a farm, the makers
took the revolutionary step of bringing in the Outside Broadcast Unit,
which normally covered sporting events, for exterior scenes. Prior to
this, soaps in Ireland and Britain had been studio-bound affairs. As a
direct result of the success of *The Riordans*, ITV launched its own rural
counterpart *Emmerdale Farm* (later plain *Emmerdale*) in 1972.

The show was so successful at imparting subliminal instruction
that the station was emboldened to start up a programme, *Teilifis*

Feirme, that addressed itself directly to teaching the do's and don'ts of farming without the window dressing of births, deaths and marriages. This freed up *The Riordans*, which remained must-see TV for the masses, to devote more airtime to exploring the social issues of the day. In doing so, the soap brought to bear the same willingness to kick out the old and bring in the new that it had applied to outdated farm practices.

The short-lived off-again-on-again romances of Benjy, the son who stood to inherit the farm if his father Tom would ever hand it on, kept audiences on tenterhooks. As the chief writer, Wesley Burroughs, reflected: 'In the case of Benjy, the mothers of Ireland have to some extent looked on him as a foster son. And like Mary [his mother], they think nobody is good enough for him.' After a number of years, Burroughs decided that it was time to marry off Benjy following no fewer than eight screen engagements.

More than one of those broken engagements had been to Maggie, whom the possessive mothers of Ireland grudgingly recognised as his soulmate. As the writer put it, Maggie had made the vital connection with the core audience and had 'been accepted by the public as the rightful and natural contender for Benjy's hand'.

But when Burroughs tried to steer the slow-moving soap a little more speedily down the aisle, he found his path blocked from on high. He developed a plot line which hinted that Maggie was getting a little more pregnant each week, although she and Benjy were still only courting. In the writer's own words, Maggie began 'displaying symptoms which the most sheltered of viewers could not mistake'. Eventually, the penny dropped with the sheltered viewers in charge of the national broadcaster and Burroughs was hauled before his employers and told he had better write his way out of trouble. He ended up paying a visit to a doctor to come up with an illness that would innocently explain away Maggie's condition.

The show then touched another raw nerve when it tackled the taboo topic of marriage break-up. Viewers reacted badly to the split between the flaky Jude Riordan and her agricultural instructor husband Jim Hyland, but things got worse when angry letters began arriving in the RTÉ mailbox after the separated wife started hanging around with a suave divorced Canadian mining executive who was hovering about surveying mineral deposits. Derek Young, the actor playing Jude's estranged husband Jim, reportedly bore the brunt of the public hostility to the unwelcome plot twist in their favourite soap. Young was touring in an unrelated stage role at the time but the performances were ruined on a nightly basis by the heckles of audience members shouting 'Go back to Jude!'

Bibliography

Akenson, Don, *An Irish History of Civilisation*, Granta.
Bielenberg, Andy (Ed.), *The Shannon Scheme*, Lilliput.
Ryan, Tim, *Tell Roy Rogers I'm Not In*, Blackwater Press.
Howard, Paul, *The Joy*, O'Brien Press.
Swift, Jonathan, *A Modest Proposal*, Penguin.
Oram, Hugh, *The Advertising Book*, MO Books.

Evening Herald
Evening Press
Hot Press
In Dublin
Irish Independent
Irish Press
The Irish Times
Magill
Sunday Business Post
Sunday Independent
Sunday Press
Sunday Times
Sunday Tribune

National Archives: Department of the Taoiseach
National Archives: Department of Agriculture
National Archives: Department of Education
National Archives: Department of the Environment
National Archives: Department of Finance
National Archives: Department of Posts & Telegraphs
National Archives: Department of Foreign Affairs
National Archives: Department of Health

Oireachtas Website: www.oireachtas.ie
Bord Fáilte Publications